eros in
la belle epoque

eros in la belle epoque

by Patrick Waldberg
Translation by Helen R. Lane

GROVE PRESS INC., NEW YORK

End papers: Drawings after Toulouse-Lautrec,
A. Rouveyre, G. Meunier, Xavier Sager, Forain,
Mars, G. Trilleau.

To Georges Salles, born with the Eiffel Tower,
this evocation of the pleasures of his elders.

Contents

1. *Danaïd*. Auguste Rodin. Musée Rodin, Paris.

❨ FOREWORD ❩

François Mauriac made this interesting remark one day: "Is the clinical study of eroticism more damnable in the eyes of God than the prudent use we novelists have made of it? The *Story of O* is chilling, of course, and I for my part cannot bear to read it; but this very horror perhaps keeps us from giving in to the sort of sexual uneasiness that was aroused in me, when I was sixteen, by expressions of tenderness and sweetness, such as in this passage from Paul Bourget's *Cruelle Enigme* [*Cruel Enigma*]: 'Ah,' she said, resting her perfumed hand on Hubert's eyelids, 'how I should like to sleep on your heart!' Who knows whether this is not worse than *The Story of O?*"[1]

In our opinion this reflection expresses a profound truth. The paths of erotic revelation are indeed, like the paths of the Lord, unfathomable. Accidents, chance meetings, harmless images that suddenly become warped, surprise comparisons, unintentional hints—anything can serve as the springboard for the libidinous imagination, which cannot submit to the world's reasons but, rather, fashions the world in accordance with its own caprices.

Children's literature, to begin with, is often suspect. Need we call to mind the confused, vague feelings of excitement that the excessively moral fables of the Countess de Ségur, née Rostopchine, have aroused in generations of very young readers? The misfortunes undergone by Sophie, the virtue of the Petites Filles Modèles [The Model Little Girls], the calvary of François-le-Bossu [François the Hunchback], the punishments undergone by the Bon Petit Diable [Good Little Devil], the perversion of Jean-qui-grogne [Grumbling John] and the rectitude of Jean-qui-rit [Laughing John] are overdramatized sensory renderings of the consequences of "good" and "bad" conduct. Sin or sanctity: both bring on a sense of dizziness. The child reader walks a tight-rope between two chasms, and his soul experiences the attraction of the abyss.

The brutal disclosure of the truth, the naked act cynically paraded may bring on horror and malaise, but allusion, furtive fondling, the "expressions of sweetness" as Mauriac puts it, saturate the mind with a more deadly poison. In like manner, it is a proven fact that the "teasers" who lead a man on, who seem to offer themselves and then take back the offer, using just the right mixture of provocation and disappointment, are much more exasperating to men than those women whose approach is direct and crude.

---

[1] "Bloc-Notes," *Le Figaro Littéraire*, February 2, 1963.

2. *Female faun in a trance.* J. B. Carpeaux. Terra cotta. Robert Lebel Collection, Paris.

3. *Vase.* Daum. Polychrome glass.   4. *Diana.* Carrier-Belleuse. 1895.

In this book we have endeavored to show how eroticism *openly* manifests itself in the three decades from 1880 to 1910 the period that has been called La Belle Epoque. We have taken care not to force the door of secret collections. Nor have we embarked upon a clinical study, and we have deliberately chosen to make no mention of the work of doctors, scientists, and psychologists whose discoveries during this period shed some light on the sexual behavior of humans. We cannot forget, however, that the last quarter of the nineteenth century saw the rise of modern sexology, marked by the inventories of Krafft-Ebing, the classifications of Havelock Ellis, and the research of Charcot on hysteria which led to Sigmund Freud's brilliant insights.

5. *Siren*. Vase.

6. *Apparition*. Artist unknown. Green earthenware. Circa 1900. Robert Lebel Collection, Paris.

7. Illustration by Aubrey Beardsley for *Made-moiselle de Maupin* by Gautier. Bibliothèque Nationale, Paris.

Our purpose here is not to analyze but to describe. It is through the every-day and the immediate, rather than the illicit and rare, that the truth of an era stands out. We have attempted to evoke an erotic climate with the visible as our point of departure, bringing to light a great number of facts which have been forgotten, but which were common knowledge in their day. Thus we have concerned ourselves principally with facts having to do with daily life, femi-nine dress and adornment, street scenes, public places, stage shows, the obvious aspects of love for sale, and sexual aberrations.

8. *Siren*. Sophie Burger-hartmann (or her school). Ashtray.

Our sources are the images handed down to us by this era: photographs, posters and advertisements, illustrations of books, old programs, covers of novels or sheet music; and also filler items in newspapers, accounts of music-hall or theater performances, chronicles of life on the boulevards and in high society, classified ads, the verses and choruses of popular songs. Literary fads, successful or scandalous novels, poetry answering to the taste of the day—these, too, have enabled us to rediscover the lines of force that time had somewhat blurred.

It is common knowledge that the name "Art Nouveau" has been given to the décor of these thirty years—a prodigious floral, sensual, shimmering, foamy flood, bearing in its wake nereids and nymphs, sirens with seaweed

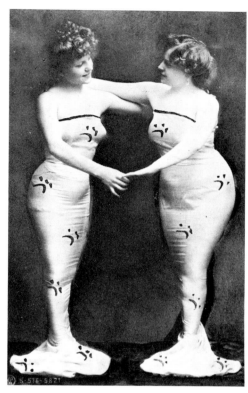

9. *Nickel-plated feet.* Three-dimensional card.

10. *Flanking the Vase,* after Albert Samain. Robert Giraud Collection, Paris.

11. *Apotheosis.* Bronze. Detail from the south group, Grand Palais, Paris.

12. *Dragonflies.* Jean Vignes Collection, Paris.

13. *Beauty with a whip.* "La Lanterne Magique"
Collection, Paris.

hair, ecstatic virgins, princesses entwined with morning glories, or androgynes
peeking out from water lilies. Here is a whole world of everyday, provocative
sensuality, a whole forest of sexual symbols, whose repeated suggestions at
length set the fashion for desire and love. The bachelor apartment of the
seducers in Paul Bourget and the boudoir of the courtesan Liane de Pougy,
the façade of the Bal Bullier in front of which Bubu de Montparnasse solicit-
ed, the colonnades of the Tivoli-Vauxhall whose gas lamps turned the faces
of Bruant's streetwalkers pale—all were afflicted with the same ornamental,
spiraloid, creeping, pistillate madness.

14. One of a portfolio of six drawings entitled
Lesbian Round Dance. Franz von Bayros.

Another characteristic phenomenon of this era is the alternation of brutal, animal realism and hazy, sometimes half-demented intellectualizing. Between the "slice of life" presented without frills—*Chair Molle* [Soft Flesh] of Paul Adam,[2] for instance, which is both an excellent book and a precious document—and the titillations of the soul of Raoule de Vénérande, the heroine of *Monsieur Vénus* by Rachilde,[3] there is, so to speak, no middle term. The end of the century is torn between these two poles: naturalism with its smell of kitchens and misery, and symbolism with its fingers weighted down by rings.

Eros in La Belle Epoque proposes to describe the joys, the sufferings, the weariness, and the tribulations of the flesh, its glorification and its mockery, in all their diverse appearances—in days when it was decked out in tulle and black Chantilly lace.

---

[2] Paul Adam, *Chair Molle* (Bruxelles: Aug. Brancart, 1884).

[3] Rachilde, *Monsieur Vénus* (Paris: Genonceaux, 1889). Published in English translation, New York: Couici, Friede, 1929.

15. *Above and Below*. G. Meunier. Drawing. 1903.

I.

FRILLS, FURBELOWS, AND FLUTTERINGS

> And I shall be the model husband
> As the rustle of your dress
> Is the model rustling.
> Jules Laforgue

The onomatopoetic word *froufrou* [rustling] was never more appropriate than in these years at the end of the century when the passage of a woman was revealed, even to the blind, by the rustle of taffetas and Liberty silks, the flutter of ruching, the light tapping of laces on a bronze hide.

Sheathed, buried, corseted, padded in multiple thicknesses that were either soft and downy or rigid and rough to the touch, the woman of this era calls to mind some mysterious chrysalis lost within a cocoon impossible to unwind. In extreme cases, nothing of her is visible, since the only parts of her body it would be permissible to view, her face and her hands, disappear, the first beneath a veil, the second in a muff or gloves.

The imagination runs on, takes wing, and sometimes loses its way in the face of this jealous cuirassing. Rather than being seen, the woman is divined—through her stature, her walk, her figure, the dimensions of her foot thrust into a boot, the cut of her cloak, the luxuriousness of her fur, the perfume that lingers in her wake. It is all a game that fires a man's thoughts and exasperates his desire.

It is not surprising that shivers run up his spine as a stair is climbed, as the raised skirt permits a furtive glimpse of snowy white underwear or the lightning flash of a black stocking, or as a slight tilt of the head allows a fleeting glance at a fragment of bare skin at the nape of the neck. Mayol, whose repertory is a fine reflection of the times, has given us this verse:

Moi, rien que d'apercevoir
Un bas noir
Le coeur me bat, c'est étrange,
Je ferais tout pour l'avoir.

[Just looking at
A black stocking
Makes my heart pound, it's strange
I'd do anything to have it.]

Flesh is so well hidden, kept so secret, that a simple ceremony of hand-kissing takes on the seriousness of a carnal embrace: the touch of a bare hand brushing a mustache is enough to bring ecstasy.

16. *In the street.* Liane de Pougy, *Myrrhile,* a Parisian novel with 14 photographic illustrations and a preface by M. W. Busnach, Nilsson, Paris, n.d. [1899].

17. *The latest fashion.*

18. *A Woman Who's Really Surrounded* (Song by Marcel-Lévêque.) *La Grande Vie,* "illustrated solely by photography based on Nature," [1901].

Muffs

Just think of the possibilities of licentiousness that this object—the muff—can offer the imagination! It is a warm nest, cradling hands that doubtless are charming, hands which come to be clasped by those of the man who desires: fingers that interweave, twine and untwine, with feverish pressures or light caresses—totally hidden from all eyes, in the absolute secrecy of the equivocal casing, while the entire body strains, trembles, clings to these exquisite feints.

"How luxurious fashionable muffs have been these last twenty years!" Octave Uzanne exclaims in 1892, and cites this appealing nomenclature from a column on fashions signed "Étincelle" (the Viscountess of Peyronny): "The Nest-Muff, in ribbed satin, lined with black and white lace, with a flock of Bengal parrots and frightened parakeets nestling in the satin folds.

"The Flower-Muff, bigger than anything, of ivory, cardinal red, or navy-blue plush, and clusters of roses, marigolds, camellias, and violets spreading their petals in the middle amid froths of lace.

"The Watteau-Muff, for evening: a circle of cupids painted on white satin; the Coppée-Muff, wet sparrows on a background of black satin; the Figaro-Muff, in black velvet, entirely covered by a lattice of black and gold chenille, [with] three humming-birds in a nest of black lace; the Duchess-Muff: all in imitation-fur marabou, scattered with little bows of flame-colored satin...."

19. *Plumed hat.*

Some of them, Uzanne also tells us, became "veritable sachets, perfumed with heliotrope, rose, gardenia, verbena, or violet, or powdered inside with orris root or Maréchale powder."[4]

Gloves

Outside the muff the hand, shy and sensitive to the cold, takes refuge in the supple and docile mold of the glove. Though it is true that in the era we are speaking of this object is not as sumptuous as it is known to have been in eras farther back in the past—such as the "perfume gloves" of the court of the Valois, silk gloves embossed with gold threads and set with precious stones of Venetian dogaressas—it nonetheless is still indispensable and still valuable as a symbol.

In a melancholy sonnet, Paul Morand remembers Marcel Proust, "wearing filoselle gloves." Old maids going to mass on Sunday, with their reticule on their wrist, wear gloves of this same material. "Gloves for daytime wear of China silk, Spanish Gloves, Gloves

[4] Octave Uzanne, *Les Ornements de la Femme* (Paris: Librairies-Imprimeries Réunies, 1892).

20. *At the races.* After *Le Panorama*, "Paris Amuses Itself," Ludovic Baschet, Paris, s.d.

21. *Female Attire.* Albert Guillaume.

customary oath. She was wearing a pair of these very same sixty-four-button gloves which she was obliged to partially unbutton, for the legal formalities required that the right hand be bare. An afternoon wasn't time enough for this, and the trial had to be adjourned to another day.

The arm, the forearm, the wrist, and above all the hand are the objects of artful unveilings, whose teasing slowness stirs desire. In *Gilda*,[6] an American film, sensuous Rita Hayworth, her arms gliding back and forth in vermilion gloves like an amorous swan, showed us all the sexual excitement that this often-sumptuous ornament is capable of arousing. Is it not a truism that as far as

[6] Directed by Charles Vidor (1945).

of beaver, suede, glazed kid, musketeer Gloves, Columbine Gloves, fencing Gloves"[5] —and the list could be extended to include tulle or lace gloves, or the long black gloves that Yvette Guilbert wore, their fluttering fixed forever by Lautrec, or even the archaic mittens to which a few aged female celebrities of the day remained faithful.

There is also talk in the gossip-columns of thirty-two-button chamois gloves which cover the arm almost to the shoulder. Taking off one's gloves thus involved sixty-four motions. One can imagine the lot of the excited lover who patiently takes on the task of unbuttoning them, placing his lips on a bit of bare skin at each step in the process of unveiling! Doubtless Jean Cocteau was thinking of a situation of this sort when he put the pre-suicide phrase "Too many buttons; I'm going to kill myself!" in the mouth of an Englishman in his *Le Grand Ecart* [The Splits], published in English under its French title.

An elegant lady, called to testify in some lawsuit or other, was asked to swear the

[5] O. Uzanne, *op. cit.*

22. *The triumph of pearls.* Arlette Dorgère and Lantelme. After *Le Gaulois du Dimanche.*

desire is concerned, everything that veils, hides, or conceals, enhances at the same time the value of what is covered up? Just as the velvet mask enhances the face through the power of the unknown, so the glove makes the hand the object of lustful desires. For at least four decades Mayol was to sing these famous words without their charm fading:

> Les mains de femme
> Je le proclame
> Sont des bijoux
> Dont je suis fou.

> [Women's hands
> So say I
> Are jewels
> That I'm mad about.]

Hats

If the glove closely follows the contours of the hand, clings to the skin, and gives an animal litheness and suppleness to the member wearing it, the hat, on the contrary, makes the body taller, prolongs it, makes it take up more space, and turns it into a poetic vision of Eden, of Never-Never Land, or of hanging gardens. If one leafs through issues of *Figaro-Graphic, La Vie Parisienne, La Nouvelle Mode, L'Illustration,* or *Le Gaulois du Dimanche* from the years between 1890 and 1910, one sees ladies' hats displayed on a great number of pages, in all their luxuriant splendor.

Whether a widow's black veils or a colonel's egrets, the flanks of birds of paradise, or rooster or ostrich feathers, a whole unreal world is built on these stiffened tulles over stretched velvet, over Italian straw—immense strands decorated with foamy, frothy materials, sometimes black and sometimes mauve or white. Sometimes the woman is dressed all in one color. This is how Jean Lorrain pictures the Bois de Boulogne on a June morning in 1895: "These immense white

23. *Brooch.* Alfons Maria Mucha. Portrait of Sarah Bernhardt. Hessiches Landesmuseum, Darmstadt.

24. *The Butterfly.* Jewelry. Eugène Feuillâtre. 1902. N. V. Citroën Collection, Amsterdam.

25. *The Initiation.* Franz von Bayros. Illustration
for *Fleurette's Purple Snails,* first publication of
the Society of Austrian Bibliophiles.

26. "La Belle Sophie."

surmounted by a bouquet meant to conceal the lady's back-combs; sometimes the tulle-bedecked straw cloche is complemented by a loop of ribbon studded with cabochons and below them a maline ruffle that caresses the hair. On toques of velvet or felt, the collarette of the great crested grebe rivals tufts of egret feathers, and the tail feathers of the lophophorus, also known as the golden bird, gleam resplendently.

Hatpins

These fragile and complex architectural structures, assembled by the mischievous fingers of milliners, are held onto the hair by the crossed shanks of a formidable instrument: the hatpin. If one of these pins is sticking out and he gets too close to the face of his beloved, the unfortunate man who

tulle hats, dripping with flowers, these dresses, whiter still...these shoes of white leather, this whole symphony in white major...."[7]

But in other seasons the rainbow reasserts its rights, and the woman's hat borrows all the subtle range of color of the most luxurious aviaries, hotbeds, gardens in Provence, prairies in summer. The lophophorus, birds of paradise, the ostrich and the vulture, the swan and the marabou, the kingfisher and the heron, the pheasant and the woodcock lend their sheen to the glamour of this permanent article of clothing.

Sometimes the open wings of a stuffed seagull are spread out so as to completely cover the oval of Japanese straw tilted over the forehead, while the nape of the neck is

27. "She looked like a shrine with a fortune invested in it...."

---

[7] Jean Lorrain, *Poussières de Paris* (Paris: Fayard, n.d.), p. 216.

brushes against her risks having his eye put out or getting badly scratched. On occasion the hatpin can become a weapon: of outraged modesty when things get unpleasant, of jealousy when it serves to stab a rival.

Like everything else that once upon a time contributed to the adornment of the female body, the head or cabochon of the hatpin was the object of refinements sometimes pushed to extremes. There are enormous pear-shaped ones made of blonde tortoise shell, others that are large baroque pearls, and still others in transparent enamel representing moths, variegated butterflies, scarabs, rose-beetles, ladybugs, and even flies. "People are fond of certain models whose branches are centered on a large stone and radiate outward in groups of stones to the edge of a circle, thus calling to mind graceful umbellifers."[8]

[8] *Le Gaulois du Dimanche,* May 14–15, 1910.

29. *The Comtesse de Castiglione.* Photograph by Adolphe Braun. Reprinted from *Le Point,* January, 1958.

Veils

Beneath the shadow of these straws or these stiffened velvets built up with rare plumes, lace, ribbons, artificial flowers and fruits, precious stones and various odds and ends, the face of the woman, her smile and her eyes, come to life. Not in any immediate way, however, for there is her veil! Without hiding her face completely this transparent bit of fabric blurs her features, makes them vague, disturbs them. The weave, which often has dots in it or is irregularly thickened here and there by a less transparent pattern, makes the whole thing look as if it were floating, the features like objects enveloped in a light fog.

Until the turn of the century the veil was quite thick, with floral patterns in Chantilly

28. *Wasp waists.* Berthe. "La Lanterne Magique" Collection, Paris.

or boas? Not at all, because for a long time yet this chaste colonnade will be caught in the fine net of a stiffened chemisette. All flesh is secret, and there is not a particle of it that such an interdiction does not accuse of concupiscence.

Jewels

A great number of naïve poems have evoked the excitement of "the first kiss through the veil" (François Coppée). But nothing can compare with the lyricism that jewelry, the supreme sign of female royalty, has inspired in all ages. The Art Nouveau jewel observes the laws of sinuous harmony of decoration in this era. We see, on a reduced scale, the same onslaughts of waves and whorls, the same horticultural fantasies, the same naiads or nymphs emerging from the gleam of precious gems.

30. Daguerrotype of French "fille de joie," circa 1870.

or Valenciennes lace, and still later the face disappeared altogether beneath the tulle thicknesses of "muffling" veils, meant to be worn out of doors. Castagnette praises these veils highly in her column,[9] but soon they go out of style, the veil becomes thinner, and transparency triumphs. There then come into use veils with large open spaces, veils woven with hexagons on a light background, and crackled tulle with inserts of graceful floral motifs, as well as the "spider" stitch imitating Renaissance embroidery. Thus the face, though not entirely bared, nonetheless becomes less timid and reveals itself little by little. Will the neck, so often described as "frail" and so frequently compared to that of a swan, emerge from high collars, shawls,

---

[9] *Monsieur et Madame*, October 19, 1905.

31. *Stockings, petticoats, and bloomers* . . . Postcard. (1896?)

32. *And the height from the knee to the hip...*
Postcard. (1896?)

> C'est la Femme aux bijoux,
> Celle qui rend fou
> C'est une enjôleuse!
>
> [It's the Woman with the jewels
>   The one who drives you mad
>   She makes them prettier still!]

This song is still heard today, usually parodied by dunces who doubtless think that today's songs are better. But the public in those days kindly allowed themselves to be moved by it.

Note what terms Jean Lorrain carefully

33. Drawing by Max Frölich.

34. Colette.

chooses to describe a pendant, in an unpublished poem cited by Henri Duvernois:[10]

Dans l'or vert émaillé de fauve des glycines,
La svelte nudité d'une nymphe apparaît,
Un orfèvre oiseleur a surpris dans un rai
De lune cette fée et, dans les pierres fines,
A fixé la chimère et sculpté le reflet,
Chair de femme et d'étoile prise au filet
   D'or d'un joyau de songe.

[In the green gold of wisteria enameled a
     tawny color
The willowy bareness of a nymph appears,
A bird-catching goldsmith surprised this fairy
In a ray of moonlight, and in fine stones
Fixed the chimera and sculptured its reflection:
The flesh of a woman and a star finally
     trapped
   In the golden net of a dream-jewel.]

From the same essay, in which Henri Duvernois proves himself an expert on jewelry without this knowledge altering the naturalness of his style, we shall quote a description of a ring belonging to Madame Cora Laparcerie-Richepin: "Three large teardrop pearls are set in mauve irises; the tear is a moonstone, that strange, impressive stone that Baudelaire would have written searching verses about—if the art of the jeweler had been that subtle in Baudelaire's time." And here is a description of the ring specially designed for the actor de Max: "Monsieur de Max's ring is awesome. It symbolizes the most tragic passage from *Prometheus*, whose liver, according to mythology, was eaten away by a vulture: the cruel talons of the bird grip a ruby, polished on one side but not the other, representing the liver; below it is a drop of coagulated blood which is an uncut ruby." Here, finally, is a ring, with a more tender source of inspiration, which belonged to Sarah Bernhardt: "It represents Lake Constance; at the bottom is a dark

sapphire, the depths of the water; at the top a light-colored sapphire; a naked naiad is nonchalantly lying on the shore."

The popular refrain was quite true:

   Mon coeur est un joujou
   Pour la Femme aux bijoux!

   [My heart is a toy
     For the Woman with the jewels!]

The demimondaines who parade in the Bois near Armenonville or at suppers at Maxim's proudly showed off their rich jewels, the trophies of triumphant femininity. In his *Souvenirs*, Hugo, the maître d'hôtel at this establishment, recounts the following anecdote:

Madame Otéro dined at Maxim's one evening, all covered with jewels, necklaces, bracelets, rings-on-the-thumb-and-other-fingers, a tiara and a spray. . . . She looked like a shrine with a fortune invested in it. . . . Madame Liane's table stayed empty. . . . Finally, Madame de Pougy appeared in a perfect black velvet dress, without a single jewel. There was a moment of surprise that changed to stupefaction when Madame Liane stood aside and unmasked her chambermaid, in a close-fitting cap. . . . She had had all her diamonds sewn onto this girl; there wasn't a square centimeter on her that was not dazzling. The Grand Duke Wladimir was open-mouthed. . . . Liane, who was escorted by the Count de T., sat down amid

35. *The Gourmand*. Painting by Maurice Besnaux (Behmer).

[10] Henri Duvernois, "Bijoux d'aujourd'hui," in *Je sais tout*, 1re Année, No. IV, May 15, 1905.

36. *Intimacy*. Henri Boutet. Engraving by Gillot.

37. Illustration by Franz von Bayros for *The Hundred New Short Stories* by Anthoine de La Sale.

frenetic bravos. Madame Otéro, furious, got up to leave and as she passed by Madame de Pougy's table could not forbear from uttering terrible swear-words in Spanish. She got a tongue angelically stuck out at her.[11]

Underwear

So this is how the woman looked—with her hat, gloves, muff, veil, pearls, and diamonds, at once dazzling and enigmatic, a sparkling lure whose gold, velvet, and watered silk multiply the charm of her secret delights. Let us open, let us peel this fruit bristling with artful complications, and thereby perhaps get to the heart of this mystery that turns the heads of a whole male population.

The minute the dress is raised or blows aside, the minute the artistically booted foot moves cautiously up onto the step of a victoria or a coupé, the tempting fleeciness of petticoats suddenly appears—"Her Majesty the Petticoat," as Armand Lanoux put it.

People of the period were very conscious of this empire, as these lines by Monsieur de

[11] Armand Lanoux, *Amours 1900* (Paris: Hachette, 1961).

Mirecour prove: "The luxuriousness of underwear, which is of prime importance to women of refinement, has taken on insane proportions in the last few years. . . . Nowadays the woman who prides herself on her elegance is not content with silk or lawn that is set off by inserts of real Mechlin or Valenciennes lace; all her underthings must match so that all its colors blend and harmonize with the dress that is to cover them."[12]

There is a refrain, one still hummed today, that sums up the era when petticoats reigned supreme:

> Froufrou, froufrou,
> Par son jupon la femme,
> Froufrou, froufrou,
> De l'homme grise l'âme . . .
>
> [Rustle, rustle,
> The woman with her petticoat
> Rustle, rustle,
> Intoxicates men's souls . . .]

Beneath the dress, beneath the skirt, a warm perfumed cloud swirls: the sly gravitational pull of underthings, whose complexity, studied elegance, and luxury have never

---

[12] *Les Dessous élégants,* October, 1901.

38. Photograph. Roger-Viollet.

39. *The Two Friends and the Corset.* H. C. White. Stereoscopic view. 1902. Chicago.

40. *Of one mind.* Postcard. Robert Giraud Collection, Paris.

known a more propitious moment. These antechambers of love hold more people than paradise itself.

Petticoats and Bloomers

The woman is like a flower turned upside down, with her petticoats as the petals. White petticoats hemmed with lace, of batiste or lawn, black or colored petticoats in taffeta, faille, Liberty silk, watered silk, bordered by

41. Illustration from a hardcover edition of *The Pearl*, an erotic magazine of Victorian England. The hardcover reissue appeared in the 1880's and was "Printed for the Society of Vice."

42. Lilly Nador's figure. Photograph by Gerlach.

of a frenzy than a daring state of nakedness would."[13]

With more perverse refinement a Marcel Prévost describes a group of high-school boys who, in order to enjoy their young abbot-prefect's confusion, lead him into a yard where the underclothes of a girls' boarding school are hanging out to dry on a clothes-line. "The bloomers," he writes, "were there, hung up by the waist; the soft breeze filled the belly and the legs, tossed them back and forth, enlarged then narrowed their opening, and the blue sky could be seen through this moving aperture."[14]

The use of bloomers, which goes back to the beginning of the nineteenth century, became more widespread in the time of crinolines and bustles. In this period they were usually made of calico, percale, or shirting, unprepossessing and modest materials, but in the last two decades of the century, in the victorious reign of Eros, they become finer and so thin that they are transparent. Let us pick at random one of the newspaper columns on Parisian elegance written by Svelt:

Satin bloomers are not as new as the black silk maillot which follows the curve of the body more faithfully. . . . Those women who are cold-blooded wear it under a broadcloth dress entirely lined with fur. . . . Black satin bloomers for street wear, and rose or white satin for evening wear, are nonetheless still in fashion . . . and it would be a serious error to believe that this use of bloomers has lessened or compromised the elegance of underthings, that famous corrupting underwear of the world of women. The underskirt is completely changed; it is replaced by a full-length lining of mousseline de soie, trimmed with ruches and lace and placed inside the dress with brush braid on the bottom that follows the supple and undulating movements [of the body].[15]

a pleated flounce: pushing aside all these delicate layers, one discovers that the double pistil of the legs is covered, above the garter that holds up the stockings, by bloomers, which in those days were known as "indispensables," "unmentionables," or "inexpressibles."

Underthings take up a fair amount of space in the literature and newspapers of the time. Here is a typical passage, from one novel out of hundreds: "Across the bed, on the faded old-rose counterpane, there can be made out the wrinkled pair of batiste bloomers that she wore, so flimsy and short, with lace frills and ribbon furbelows, one of those pairs of bloomers that fail to reach down past the lace garters, that put a lover in more

[13] René Maizeroi, *L'Adorée* (Paris: Havard, 1887).

[14] Marcel Prévost, "L'Abbé Pantalon," in the *Gil Blas Littéraire,* December 24, 1890.

[15] *La Vie Parisienne,* January 14, 1899.

Shedding Their Petals

In this period, which it would not be too much of a paradox to call the "underwear era," an important part of the life of women —those progeny of batiste—was spent dressing and undressing. Novelists willingly linger on the details of these major operations:

Alphonsine then put on her corset, a black corset with fan-shaped gores in yellow silk, and her stockings, long flesh-colored stockings that clung to her calves. She took from the mirrored armoire a bodice of red calico trimmed in marabou, and a skirt of the same color with four rows of edging in gold. . . . She put on her bloomers, supporting herself on the edge of the bed with her foot on a chair. They were trimmed with lace insertions and embroidery and closed at the top with a ribbon. Then she tied her bustle on in back and put on a little petticoat in blue flannel with a broad band of lace and on top of it a second petticoat of watered silk trimmed with velvet.[16]

[16] Auguste Tabarant, *Virus d'amour* (Brussels: Kistemaeckers, 1887).

44. A horsewoman's corset.

43. *The corset. La Vie Parisienne.*

Other authors even go so far as to leave out the presence of women altogether, believing it enough of an aphrodisiac to simply describe underthings scattered here and there: "His cerebellum was assailed by the female odor that hung over the room, a sharp blonde odor, made all the sharper by the irritating mixture of perfumes with which Gabrielle for some weeks had been scenting her underthings. And these underthings were strewn about everywhere; her stockings here, next to the chemise in a white pile on the floor, crumpled into a thousand fine little wrinkles and damp under the arms, with its lace all curled up and stained several colors by her dress; her skirt there, with her petticoats still half puffed out; and her collapsed bloomers with their crumpled legs lying flat. . . ."[17]

[17] Léo Trézenik, *Cocquebins* (Paris: Monnier, 1887).

38

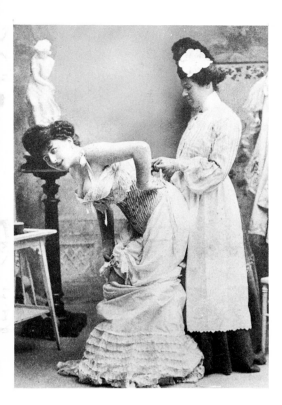

45. *Lina d'Arteuil's Corset.* Photograph by Guenda, Marseille.

This literature merely translates, more or less resourcefully, the constant preoccupations of the "decadent turn of the century." A whole system of permanent suggestion turns the male's mind toward these disturbing fluffy nests that women's underthings represent. Even in the street the stroller cannot escape the provocation of suggestive underwear, as these lines, taken from a society column by Mitton, prove: "A large lingerie shop displayed, around 1900, the magnificent trousseau of an aristocratic young Parisienne who was soon to be united in marriage to a happy fiancé. Now all the nightdresses—a great many of them, trimmed in fine lace—had a slit, three to four inches long and coquettishly bordered in delicate lace, just below the hips in the middle of the front."[18]

With these muslins, these batistes, these

46. *The "Lysiane" Corset,* by A. Claverie.

[18] *Les Dessous élégants,* May, 1901.

48. *The "Perfection" Corset,* by A. Claverie.

47. *A turn of the screw....*

satins, this Irish or Mechlin lace—beribboned, buttoned, hooked, laced—turning the woman of 1900 into a baby-doll occupies the clever hands of legions of lingerie-seamstresses, embroiderers, pleaters, or lace-makers. These are fairy hands, well-suited to the task of spinning gossamer webs, to which we owe those ephemeral masterpieces of the sort that Ghilda describes as "modern" underwear: "A daytime chemise and bloomers in white batiste decorated with sky-blue batiste trimming which is quite new, and edged with openwork insertions. The chemise is gathered at

49. *The Dressing Room.* Toulouse-Lautrec.

to a sea anemone or to a jellyfish cradling its transparencies and its feeding filaments in the waves. But our tableau is missing one essential element, the hard part, the cuirass whereby this provocative mollusk will take on the proud and aggressive appearance of the lobster, of the phyllomorph bedbug, of the lucanus or stag-beetle: this nielloed, damascened dream-armor is the corset.

After having recognized the aptness of Armand Lanoux's expression "Her Majesty the Petticoat," we have had second thoughts and the desire, now that we have the supporting documents in hand, to downgrade this accessory in favor of the corset, on which we shall bestow the title of "Her Imperial Majesty." In all truth, each of these pieces of finery has its function: the one entices and teases, the other fortifies and holds out.

the waist in soft pleats, and a sky-blue taffeta ribbon passes through lace eyelets. Very fine white embroidery at the top of the chemise and, forming a very wide flounce at the bottom of the bloomers, tiny, very fine little pleats between lace insertions, with ribbons and sky-blue taffeta on the shoulders, and aiguillettes of chased antique silver."[19]

While we are about it, let us praise the impeccable precision of this description whose technical exactness does not interfere at all with its evocative power: one need only close one's eyes, and the woman is there, all decked out, offered to the delights of the imagination.

Corsets

As we have seen her up to this point, haloed in the filmy softness of her flattering underthings, the woman might be compared

[19] *Les Dessous élégants,* October, 1901.

50. *The Tightest of Corsets.* Esbey.

51. *The Beauty Retiring.* 1890. *La Vie Parisienne.*

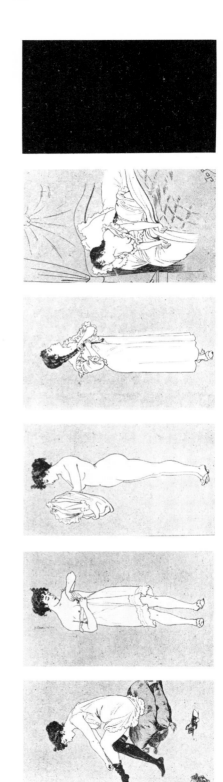

52. *The Beauty Retiring: from rolling her stockings to darkness.*

53. *Mademoiselle de Maubranche.* Photograph by Ogerau. *Le Panorama, op. cit.*

On looking at the matter more closely, however, the corset perhaps had a more important place in the erotic mythology of the woman than any other article of clothing, if only because of the tortures piously endured by those who wore them.

The bastard forms of this contraption—girdles and waist-cinchers—that we know today do not give any idea of what these merry-go-round or horse-race trappings were like in the old days. Pictures of them that leave us wool-gathering come down to us in advertisements of the period: the "Dream" corset, the "Phryne" corset, the "Mystery" corset, the "Persephone" corset, the "Josyane" corset, and many others, offered for sale by Delmirotte, Picard et Minier, Claverie, Pemjean, Guendré, or Léoty—this latter having written, lyrically and regularly, the corset-column in one of the most instructive pub-

54. *The Beauty Corseted, or Callipygian Adeline.* Henri Manuel. Photograph. 1900. After *La Grande Vie, op. cit.*

lications on the subject that 1900 has bequeathed to us: *Les Dessous élégants* [Elegant Underthings].

One's mind wanders nostalgically through these gallant vestiges: "A corset with ribbons or stiffened lace gorgets, held lightly on the shoulders by satin straps; a bolero corset in white or mauve Pekin satin or a corset in cardinal satin, trimmed with brocaded muslin forming a shawl and knotting in the middle in an elegant cravat; a corset and petticoat in ibis-pink taffeta embroidered with convolvuluses of black Chantilly lace, with insets of pink muslin through which there can be seen the deep tucks of muslin on the petticoat, ending in a ribbon of pink muslin in a cloud of black muslin."[20]

No practical obstacle manages to temper the imagination, the inventiveness, and the ingeniousness of these prodigious divas of the needle, the corsetieres: "Is there anything more graceful," Madame Léoty writes, "than

[20] *Les Dessous élégants,* coll.

55. *The solitude of Liane de Pougy.* After *I am Beautiful* by Victorien du Saussay, ed. by Albert Méricant, s.d.

56. *Evening shoes. Le Gaulois du Dimanche.*

57. *The little snob's pince-nez.* Amateur photograph. 1900. Robert Giraud Collection, Paris.

45

58. *At the Palais du Trocadero, Paris, 1878.* Roger-Viollet.

this branch of wild Bengal roses whose separate motifs can be arranged so as to adjust the spread of the branch to the special silhouette of the happy mortal for whom this adorable corset is destined?"

When it was pliable and of modest dimensions, pinching in a waist that was nicely formed by nature, the corset often was as exquisite as a jewel-box, all the more preciously ornamented when its owner treasured what it contained. But there were also carcan-corsets, designed as sumptuously as coats-of-arms, which kept the body as rigid as a tree-trunk.

Colette's memories are precious proofs of this: "Fashion gave the theater itself a bad time of it," she writes, "in this era of huge corsets that raised the bosom, lowered the hips, and hollowed the belly. Germaine Gallois, of the Variétés, an inflexible bulwarked beauty, accepted no 'sitting' roles. Sheathed

in a corset that began under the armpits and ended down around the knees, with two flat iron springs in the back, two others along the haunches, and a 'tirette' [curtain-cord] between the legs (I am using the vocabulary of the time) holding this contraption together, and with lacings, moreover, that required a lace six yards long, she was on her feet, intermissions included, from eight-thirty to midnight."[21]

Getting out of the corset, an operation which demanded both know-how and patience, inspired parodies by cabaret and music-hall performers that were invariably a hit. In his moving *Paris 1900*, a film that "aficionados" never tire of seeing over again, Nicole Védrès has revived a short in which

---

[21] Colette, *Mes apprentissages* (Paris: Ferenczi, 1936). Translated into English as *My Apprenticeships* by Helen Beauclerk (London: Secker and Warburg, 1957).

59. *The First Kiss* [top] and *The Last Kiss* [bottom]. Postcards.

47

60. English corset advertisement, 1899.

the young Maurice Chevalier artfully devotes himself to this racy act. Though the Art Nouveau corset began to disappear around 1912, the audience in neighborhood music halls had the chance to applaud, as late as 1939, the aging, obese comedian Poulot in a turn he never changed whose high point— a glaring anachronism—was "the demi-mondaine retiring for the night." The paleontological climax of this exhibition came when Poulot mimed, with hilarious contortions, the acrobatic unhooking and unlacing of the corset, followed by great sighs of relief and endless scratching of his belly and flanks.

Clowning being the other side of the coin, the inevitable complement, of royalty—as Sir James George Frazer has taught us—such mockery on the stage does nothing to destroy the sovereign dignity of the woman of 1900. She is the queen who reigns supreme, both by the sumptuousness of her appearance, which makes her a somewhat isolated, forbidden being, and by the mixed feelings of attraction and fear she inspires—the very feelings that characterize sacred personages.

In his delightful *Portraits-Souvenir*, Jean

61. *The Toilette.* Amateur photograph. Robert Giraud Collection, Paris.

Cocteau came up with this maxim: "Poetry is exactitude." He himself did not fail to display this virtue when he evoked for us the end of a century that he lived through as a child and the dawn of the next that he lived through as a young man. It is to him that we owe the most striking, and beyond a doubt the truest image of this Art Nouveau woman whose weapons we have just summarily inventoried.

"I myself, I who am speaking to you," Cocteau writes, "saw Otéro and Cavalieri lunching at Armenonville. It was nothing tossed off lightly. With their armor, shields, carcans, girdles, whalebones, piping, epaulieres, leg-guards, thigh-pieces, gauntlets, corselets, halters of pearls, bucklers of feathers, shoulder-belts of satin, velvet and gems, coats of mail, these knights bristling with tulle, spikes, and eyelashes, these sacred scar-

62. *The Sandman* (Caroline Otero). Photograph by Reutlinger.

63. *La Goulue.* J. M. Capuletti Collection, Paris.

64. One of a series of drawings entitled *Liebe*. Michael von Zichy.

abs armed with asparagus-tongs, these Samurai of sable and ermine, these cuirassiers of pleasure that were harnessed and caparisoned, at dawn, by robust ladies' maids, seemed, as they stiffly faced their host, to be able to get out of an oyster nothing less than a pearl. ... The idea of undressing one of these ladies was a costly undertaking that had better be arranged in advance, like moving a household, and to picture them in the middle of a disorder of underwear, hair, and sprawling limbs, we must have enough imagination to picture the scandal of a bedroom in which murder has been committed."[22]

The entire mind and all the senses of the male will for several years be fixated, strained,

[22] Jean Cocteau, *Portraits-Souvenir* (Paris: Grasset, 1935).

exasperated by this moving, flag-bedecked citadel, that it is perhaps less a question of brutally conquering than of surreptitiously taking its intimate succulence by surprise.

We have described in detail the refinements and the richnesses, the snares and traps that make up the arsenal of seduction. The dénouement of this tantalizing parade, when it takes place, does so in the shadow of the bedroom, amid heavy drapery, divans, cushions, moisture-beaded vases and figures draped in bronze, in the feeble light of lamps shaded with tulle.

Les longs rideaux de blanche mousseline
Que la lueur pâle de la veilleuse
Fait fluer comme une vague opaline
Dans l'ombre mollement mystérieuse ...

[The long white muslin curtains
 Shimmer in the pale light of the night-lamp
 Like a vague opaline
 In the softly mysterious shadow ...]

These were the words of Paul Verlaine, immortalizing the chiaroscuro of love-chambers. In the soft light the man, feverish and impatient, awaits the instant when the woman will bare herself in her opulent and pearly nakedness, the queen whose body, at the point of ideal perfection, takes on the fateful form of the hour-glass.

65. *The Unbreakable Corset.*

51

66. *The Bather.* Louis Chalon (1866-1915). Robert Lebel Collection, Paris.

II.

CUPID LURKING IN THE SHRUBBERY

Cahin-caha,
Hue-dia, hop là!
LEON XANROF

Like the ornithologist in the heart of the Papuan jungle spying on the habits of birds of paradise, we have just watched, standing stock-still, the spreading of the sumptuous plumage with which the woman, between 1890 and 1910, enhances her splendor.

We are now going to move our stiff joints, take on the role of a "hiker," and follow the temptress as she chances to meet people in places her footsteps will lead us to: in the street, on the boulevard, at the theater, at a ball, at a traveling show, at the water's edge, on a promenade, in the Bois. . . .

In the evening of the other century as in the morning of this one, the paths of desire were tortuous, laid out with obstacles and stopping-places, signals and ambushes. It was not permitted to go straight for the target, to allude to possession, the sexual act, any more than the body was allowed to be bared.

When Zola depicted a working girl losing her virginity in the galleries of a ruined mine (*Germinal*) or peasants coupling on the ground like their cattle (*La Terre*), modesty was outraged. Some will say that this was hypocrisy, but what period does not have its own brand of it?

It is a known fact, moreover, that Zola's violence and freedom as regards sex were not particularly appreciated by the fervent public his humanitarian ideas attracted. As it happens, the naturalist "bombshell" had a lasting effect only by virtue of the interdictions that it attempted to shatter and that survived it.

In all truth, it is restraint and modesty that make the search for erotic pleasures so attractive in the "age of underwear." The least little glimpse of a bit of the forbidden fruit becomes an object of delight, and that which provokes and defies common morality stirs the masses.

67. *The Pierced Coin.* Fox. Postcard. Jean Vignes Collection, Paris.

SOUVENIR DE PARIS

68. *The July Column*. Xavier Sager. Postcard.

The senses and sexual appetite play hooky, stimulated less by the prospect of engaging in the sexual act than by its preliminaries, less moved by the nakedness of a model, even a sublime one, than by the glimpse of a centimeter of pink flesh between the garter and the flounce of the bloomers when a lady happens to fall.

The Petticoat School

In this period everything is allusion, double-entendre, insinuation, suggestion, and symbol. The city's monuments lend themselves to the most scabrous interpretations. The July column, the Vendôme column, and the Obelisque are phallic symbols, and the Eiffel Tower's prestige surpasses theirs.

A typical image is the postcard "Souvenir of Paris" by Xavier Sager, which represents the place de la Bastille with the column in the middle, surmounted by Genius. On the head of the winged god, balancing on the toe of her boot, is a young woman flinging a leg sheathed in black in the air and thus disclosing petticoats, bloomers, and garters, while all around the fake frame of the scene is a garland of heads in opera hats, with mustaches, beards, and monocles, and the open-eyed, lubricious stare of the voyeur.

For many, sauntering about means lying in ambush. With his nostrils flaring, his eyes narrowed, the stroller lies in wait for the incident that will give him a glimpse of

69. *Our Dressmaker Girls in the Twentieth Century*. G. Mouton. Science fiction in 1896.

heaven: the awkward step that will bring a fall, the dressmaker's errand-girl pulling up a stocking that has worked loose from her garter, the milliner's helper who relaces her boot, the street-fight in which women's bodices yawn open, the scene between husband and wife or lovers climaxed by a spanking. Attention at the end of the century is fixed not on the face but under the petticoat. No era, doubtless, paid more attention to what happens at the heart of filmy lingerie or the neck-opening of bodices. Poems, novels, short stories, essays, pamphlets, songs never tire of describing the episodes in the petticoat saga. Here are some examples, found in our notes at random: Paul Marcal, *Leurs Panta-* *lons* [Their Bloomers]; Armand Silvestre, *Les Dessous de la Femme* [Women's Underwear], *Le Pantalon d'Héloïse* [Héloise's Bloomers], *La Chemise à travers les âges* [The Chemise Down Through the Ages]; John Grand-Carteret, *Le Décolleté et le Détroussé à travers les âges* [Low Necklines and Loose Undergarments Down Through the Ages]; Raoul Ponchon, *Le Pantalon* [Bloomers]; Jules Jouy, *Le Pantalon de la Goulue* [La Goulue's Bloomers]; Catulle Mendès, *Jupe courte, Robe montante* [Short Skirts, High-Necked Dresses]; Carolus Brio, *Le Pantalon de Luce* [Luce's Bloomers]; Willy and Curnonsky, *Chausettes pour Dames* [Women's Hose]; Henri Beauclair, *Le Pant-*

70. *A happy accident—for some people.*

71. *The Torn Panties.* G. Mouton. Postcard.

alon de Madame Desnou [Madame Desnou's Bloomers]; Rachilde, *Les Dessous* [Underthings], etc. . . .

Open or Closed?

The mind of the man in the street willingly torments itself with such pressing questions as: open bloomers? closed bloomers? or no bloomers at all?

Closed "indispensables" are hardly worn except by little girls, and even a goodly number of these dispense with them: "Yes, papa dear, I would like it very much if you would send me closed bloomers, because when we play with my little playmates, in the garden or on a promenade, drawing designs on the ground, with all of us gathered round in a circle, they all show their little Jesus, without blushing, look at each other's, and throw sand on it."[23]

For older girls, closed bloomers are the sign of careful upbringing and the guarantee of good conduct. Yvette Guilbert, the queen of suggestiveness, with impeccable diction, sings their praises in these terms:

[23] Antonin Reschal, *Pierette en pension* (Paris: Albin Michel, 1904).

72. *It's cold.* A. Willette. Engraving by Bordier.

73. *At the Moulin de la Galette.* 1903.

Ell' n'voulait pas avant l'mariage,
Quitter ses pantalons fermés;
Ça vous prouv' bien qu'elle était sage,
Sa mère ayant su la former.[24]

[Before marriage she didn't want to
  Forsake her closed bloomers;
  That proves to you she was really a good girl,
  Her mother having known just how to bring her up.]

When she reaches the age for love, the young girl exchanges her socks and short dresses for long skirts and hose, and closed bloomers are replaced by open ones, for obvious reasons of convenience. It is hard indeed to imagine a woman in all the tousle of her petticoats, her corset, in the jumble

[24] Cellarius, "Le Petit Modèle," in *Gil Blas illustré*, October 30, 1892.

Other authors are even more vehement, as witness this diatribe of Ernest d'Hervilly: "I shall not speak of bloomers; I hate them. They are useful, I know.... Nonetheless, they are hideous. Never wear them in the country. Women imagine that all insects are jealous of their charms. They are wrong: their charms have no intrainsectival value. Fine calico is a frontier. No more customs-duties!"[26]

In the Name of the Law

What happens underneath a skirt, when the street is the place where it happens, falls within the province of justice. Tribunals occasionally have to hand down decisions in thorny cases, in which the judges, their gravity put to the test, must devote themselves to gallant arbitration. We shall cite the case

[26] Ernest d'Hervilly, *Timbale d'histoires à la parisienne* (Paris: Marpon et Flammarion, 1883).

74. "Pansies are for thoughts—of you." Postcard. Jean Vignes Collection, Paris.

of her underwear, constrained to undo a hermetic protection when the urgent need arose, whereas with open bloomers simply hiking them up sufficed.

Among men in particular bloomers had passionate detractors. Catulle Mendès, among others, never lets the opportunity go by to déride this frustrating object: "It must be believed that Berengère especially coveted the cherries on the farthest branches, for she climbed farther out on the shaking ladder; and there was a strong gust of wind; and *as she was not one of those girls who dishonor the intimacies of the feminine toilet by virile accoutrements* [italics ours], her swain had the vision of almost the whole of a naked nymph in a flash of pink snow."[25]

[25] Catulle Mendès, *Trois Chansons* (Paris: Frinzine, 1886).

75. "Your mother doesn't make you wear closed bloomers any more?" "Of course not! I'm sixteen today!"

76. *The Bois de Boulogne . . . 102 in the shade.*
Xavier Sager. [Today one often meets patrols
with police dogs there....]

of a certain Mademoiselle Elisa, who was
given an authoritative spanking in full day-
light by Monsieur F., rue Maubée. Elisa
brought a complaint, and offered to prove
to the police commissioner "that she had
been actually *stared at* by bystanders, since
she was not wearing bloomers."[27] Monsieur
F. was found guilty of disorderly conduct.

A happening of the same sort came up
for a hearing in Orléans. A schoolteacher
from Olivet, in the straggling village of
Loiret, was the object of public castigation
on the part of a certain Monsieur Veinard,
a druggist in the same town. There was
much talk, and the schoolteacher brought a
complaint. The persecuting druggist, however, got out of it cheaply—with a mere
200-franc fine—because his victim *was wearing closed bloomers.* A columnist in the
Figaro drew the moral of this story: "Please
appreciate this amazing circumstance: the

[27] *L'Intransigeant,* April 8, 1888.

77. *Proportioned skirts, 1900.* Louis Morin.

78. *A night restaurant in Montmartre.* Xavier Sager.

79. *Here it is, dear master....* A. Willette.

irritated hand of the druggist of Olivet had encountered one of those articles of clothing that English modesty would not allow to be named. In short, the schoolteacher was wearing...bloomers. Thus in the face of this rampart of fine fabric, fluted on the bottom, tightly closed at the waist, and hermetically sealed all over, the indiscreet eyes of those who witnessed the scene got absolutely nothing for their trouble."[28]

Better than books, these little reports give us information about a state of mind that many people today find difficult to understand. It was to take years, in the eyes of people who stood firmly on principle, for the wearing of women's bloomers, which at first were considered provocative, to at last be accepted as a *seemly* practice.

In like manner, the stubborn reserve of the public made it hesitate for a long time before admitting that such care of the body

[28] *Le Figaro*, April, 1879.

L'habitude est une seconde nature.

80. *Naughty, naughty....* Xavier Sager. Postcard.

sudden show of white." At certain hours, on certain lines, it is always the same passengers who get on—at the noon lunch hour, when the stores close—and with a gleam in their eye, brushing up their mustaches, they await the baring of a calf or else the fleecy whirl at the knee of a pair of bloomers.

There are also those who are disabused: "The climb down off the bus [is] not often suggestive: just worn boots, alpaca petticoats, red flannel bloomers...unless the woman isn't wearing any," Vallet sadly comments.[29]

The grave question of omnibuses is not raised just in France. Thus we read this edifying piece of information signed Falstaff

[29] *La Vie Parisienne*, March 24, 1894.

as tub baths, showers, or the use of the bidet was fitting for people other than hetaerae, demimondaines, and ladies of the evening—those who make a public show of debauchery and sell their bodies.

Under the Skirt

Under the skirt: the joy of men on the platform of a bus eyeing a young woman climbing in. "Men on the platform [constitute] a particular type of passenger," a columnist of the *Gil Blas* writes. "They carry their investigation far beyond the knee," and thus, the same author adds, it is necessary "to provide oneself with bloomers, whose legband may sometimes timidly come into view, or else the skirt gets caught and there is a

81. *La Goulue.* Robert Giraud Collection, Paris.

82. *Girls fishing . . . before, during, and after.*
F. Chamouin. Postcard. 1897.

83. "You're going to catch cold, mademoiselle.
Will you permit me to cover you with kisses?"
"Le Petit Buffon." A. Rouveyre.

84. *An Affair of Honor.* Painting by Emile Bayard. Fred and Jo Mazzulla Collection, Denver.

(Victorien du Saussay): "News written us from Berlin: The police, who had always refused omnibuses permission to admit women on the coaches, have finally authorized them to do so. They require that the steps be wide and shielded on the side facing the public. The proposal of Dr. Hancke, asking that bloomer-skirts be required of ladies riding buses, was turned down."[30]

Another source of enticing visions is the position astraddle, in which pulled-up skirts unveil unexpected charms. Bicycles, carrousels, donkey rides on Sunday in the country occupy a choice place in the iconography of the time.

Bicycling

The costume of the "cyclewoman" was doubtless the first step that was taken toward the masculinization of feminine dress and, therefore, toward the emancipation of women. For the first time the woman "wore the pants"—cycling pants, to be sure, certain inconveniences of which soon became evident. Thus newspapers in 1897 hail the appearance of "fore-deck trousers," borrowed from the navy and said to be "as ingenious as they are decent, and as comfortable as they are elegant."[31]

Be that as it may, the passion for the bicycle, "the little queen," and the often-deliberate absent-mindedness of its lady users continue to cause daring spectacles and risqué comments. "On Sunday evening near Auvers-sur-Oise," a special reporter writes, "I met a very realistic but extremely shocking young woman who was pedaling in batiste bloomers...not even closed by a grape leaf."[32]

On occasion the law intervenes. "The Eighth Correctional Court yesterday sentenced Mademoiselle Lanjallée, charged with disorderly conduct, to a week in prison.... This young person, whose magnificent frizzed hair surrounds her head like a halo, found nothing better to do than to cover the distance between the quai Malaquais and Saint-Germain-des-Prés perched on a bicycle, with her skirts tucked up, no bloomers, and nothing but socks on her legs."[33]

A tireless observer, Jean Lorrain with his winged pen records, not without some melancholy, the recent rise of the bicycle. In his column of June 11, 1895, he writes: "Wearing wide bouffant bloomers of gray muslin, topped by the tightly-laced bust of a narrow

[33] *L'Echo de Paris*, October 10, 1898.

85. *The Swallow.*

[30] *Le Fin de Siècle*, November 12, 1896.
[31] *Le Journal*, December 9, 1897.
[32] *Le Vélo*, July 27, 1893.

jacket of white piqué belted in tawny leather, is a rather tall blonde, with a ravishing figure. With a shirt-front like a man's, in mauve batiste, the lady flaunts a white piqué cravat under a turn-down collar buttoned with a large sapphire; a complicated pattern in diamonds and sapphires runs around her belt, and with a black straw hat with a ribbon of white moire perched on her head, she shows off the slim legs of a Diana, molded by black silk stockings."

The painter of "Fards et Poisons" [Rouge and Poisons] lingered over the description of this elegant creature, whose equivocal air does not displease him at all. Nonetheless, this free, conspicuous comportment worries him. However "modern" he would like to be, he is of another time and sighs: "There are a good two or three hundred of them every morning, tomboys and teasers, who come to take their 'oats' either at the Cycle Chalet or at Armenonville, their hand resting on the rims of their 'wheel.' Everywhere, both in the Bois and on the outer boulevards, the bicycle is triumphant, but I confess that I'm old hat. How I miss the days of horsemen and horsewomen!"[34]

In the Country

The joy of bucolic Sundays in the brush at Barbizon or at the farm of somebody-or-other is the donkey ride. It is the pretext for enjoyable falls, calculated in advance by far-sighted simperers. "But did I at least fall well?" an unseated lady rider slyly asks. "Oh, admirably, my dear! We didn't know you had such pretty Valenciennes lace!" a lady-friend bittersweetly replies.

Near the knotty-pine table where they have an afternoon snack—a bowl of fresh milk and a slice of buttered whole-wheat bread—rapturous little cries go up in time to the gracious swoops of the swing, toward which stiff-collared necks crane. It seems that the women are magically aware of "the strangely attractive charm exerted on the exacerbated nerves of the male by the sight of pretty legs emerging, white and satiny,

[34] Jean Lorrain, *op. cit.*

86. *The Quadrille at the Elysée-Montmartre.* F. Lunel. Engraving by Charles Decaux. *Le Courrier Français.*

87. *"Oh, what a Pretty-like Place!"* from *Tales of the Dressing Table,* portfolio with fifteen drawings and a frontispiece, by Franz von Bayros.

from the rustlings of batiste and lace, standing out in profile, naked and unimpeded, as the swing unexpectedly reverses direction, against the inside of the petticoat in pink satin, in a line interrupted only by some furbeloweld garter."

Country Picnics: a film directed by Jean Renoir,[35] perfectly and movingly photographed by Élie Lotard, has restored their charms of yesteryear. Sylvia Bataille, lulled by the swing, draws the attention of a somber seminarian to it for a moment, and his sidelong glance creeps up under her petticoats. This fleeting bit-player, looking exactly like a wicked priest, was the well-known writer Georges Bataille.

By contrast to these "intimist" joys, the Seine and its banks, with their baths, their popular dance halls and outdoor restaurants, urge people on to franker pleasures. The "Point du Jour," the "white dawn of Paris," and its somewhat questionable diversions were celebrated by Verlaine:

Le bonneteau y fleurit "dessur" la berge,
La bonne tôt s'y déprave . . .
Comme il est joli le paysage!
Paris au loin, triste et gai, fol et sage . . .
Puis la verdure et le ciel et les types,
Et la rivière obscène et molle, avec
Des gens trop beaux, leur cigare à leur bec . . .[36]

[The three-card trick flourishes on the bank,
The housemaid soon becomes depraved
    here . . .
How pretty the countryside always is!
Paris in the distance, sad and gay, foolish and
    wise . . .
Then the greenery and the sky and the guys,
And the river obscene and soft, with
Overly handsome fellows, their cigars in their
    beaks . . .]

[35] *La Partie de Campagne,* 1940.

[36] Paul Verlaine, *Parallèlement* (Paris: Vanier, 1889). This poem had appeared previously in the review *Lutèce,* 1885.

88. *Juliette Marval does the splits.* Moulin-Rouge.

89. "Mademoiselle Bardou, who has a very senatorial name, exhibits the ample mystery of her black stockings bravely and triumphantly." Photograph by Reutlinger.

But the most colorful spot, dear to the impressionists, is the Grenouillière [the Frog-pond] near Chatou—an appropriately named island, for here many embraces begin, and grow longer and longer. Boaters glide by in their punts, their pedal-boats, their gigs, bathers splash about in the muddy water, and at night there is dancing, with girandoles and garlands and Chinese lanterns whose reflections dot the water in the distance. "Despite the immense trees overhanging the floating establishment," Maupassant writes, "despite the closeness of the water, the place was suffocating. The emanations from spilled drinks mingled with the smell of bodies and the scent of very strong perfume that saturates the skin of women of pleasure and was evaporating in this furnace. But beneath all these diverse odors there floated a light aroma of rice powder that sometimes disappeared and then reappeared, that always came back again, as if some concealed hand had shaken an invisible powder-puff in the air."[37]

[37] Guy de Maupassant, *La Femme de Paul.*

66

In the thick woods couples who have met by chance touch each other and embrace; little cries, laughter, sighs are heard as the festivities go on at the dance: "People were dancing; the couples capered about madly, face to face, throwing their legs in the air as high as the nose of their partners. The females, who had become unjointed at the hips, leaped about, enveloped by their underwear. Their feet came up above their heads ...and they swung their bellies, wriggled their haunches, shook their breasts, spreading about them the powerful smell of sweating women."

This sketch that Maupassant gives us of a dance at the Grenouillière goes beyond anecdote. It serves to describe most of the popular balls of the end of the century where the frenzy of the high-kick reigns—that spreading of petals feverishly spied on by those fascinated by the calyx. Among the mingled odors of datura, ylang-ylang, or sandalwood, alternating with the smell of overheated bodies, eyes light up when the quadrille forms, between the waltz and the polka.

The Quadrille

Already fashionable during the Second Empire, this dance—half an exhibition, half

90. The Five Semi-virgins. Le Panorama, op. cit.

67

an acrobatic performance—will remain the indispensable spice of public dance halls until the turn of the century. Hippolyte Taine has left us this sketch of an aged can-can dancer, Mariette, whom he saw at a neighborhood dance hall: "A swarthy complexion, a large waist, thin however, but all muscle. She raises her leg above her head, she has drawers on. As she dances she raises her skirts by the handful."[38]

Following in the footsteps of "Thomas Graindorge," who will later be Monsieur Taine of the French Academy, the Goncourt brothers also seek out one of the faces of

[38] *La Vie Parisienne,* April 4, 1863.

91. Mademoiselle Simier: "Who will dare to look at her legs?" Photograph by Reutlinger.

their time in popular dance halls. We owe this valuable description to them: "Opposite the orchestra a quadrille formed, immediately surrounded by all the people there, drawn by the sight of the only pretty woman in the dance hall, a Jewess, a young Herodias, a flower of Parisian perversion, a marvelous example of those shameless young girls who sell letter-paper in foggy streets. And as she stretched her leg up straight and one saw for an instant, at the height of people's heads, a turned-up tip of a boot and a lower calf in a pink stocking, her partner displayed, in a frenetic can-can, all the vulgarity of the nineteenth-century plebeian."[39]

La Goulue

Some twenty years later, it was the reign of La Goulue, whose long popularity attracted a very mixed public, roisterers and artists, night-people and poets, students and streetwalkers, all waiting for this tireless "character" to cut loose. The show was no doubt worth waiting for, if we can believe the convincing description of a journalist who today has been forgotten: "Her arms rise, unmindful of the indiscretions of the shoulder strap that takes the place of a sleeve, her legs bend, dangle, beat the air, threaten hats, drawing all eyes below her petticoats, thieving eyes that seek out the hoped-for, but ever-fleeting gaping of her embroidered bloomers. Following the progressive figures of the quadrille, the provocative bumps of her belly are followed by the lascivious grinds of her hips; her whirling skirts, nimbly raised, unveil her spread legs through the froth of pleats, emphasizing, in the rapid fall of lace, a little patch of genuine bare skin above the garter. And from this morsel of pink flesh a torrid shower of molten steel shoots out toward the panting spectator.

[39] *Journal des Goncourts,* t. II, February 9, 1863.

Then, feigning a vulgar climax of passion, this bacchante of the gutter, with her skirts brusquely tucked up to her belly, gives the circle pressing round her their fill of the sight of her curves, so thinly veiled by the transparent lace insertions that at a certain point the most intimate efflorescence is revealed by a dark patch."[40]

Let us thank this Rodriguez: what the inspired pencil of Lautrec could not attain, condemned as it was to capturing only the fleeting lightning of a scene forever fixed in its motionless splendor, Rodriguez gives us:

[40] P. Rodriguez, "Les Excentricités de la danse," special number of *Gil Blas,* May 10, 1891.

93. *A gentlewoman of the period.* Grove Press Collection, New York.

92 *The Flower Opens.* Alastair. 1905.

a plausible idea of La Goulue in action. Her real name was Louise Weber; she had got her start at the Debray dance hall, the ancestor of the Moulin de la Galette, which was frequented by bands of painters, workers' families, prostitutes, and pimps, who at that time were called "alphonses" after a character in Alexandre Dumas *fils.* In this dance hall an infernal uproar and quadrilles took the place of polkas and waltzes. Grille d'Égout [Sewer Grating], Valentin le Désossé [Valentin the Man with No Bones], la Môme Fromage [Kid Cheese], and Louis d'Or [Golden Louis] also got their start there.

94. *French Can-Can.* Ellis.

Dance Halls

Possessed of an eroticism much more aphrodisiac than the strip tease of today, this spectacle, in spite of—or perhaps because of —its vulgar side, and doubtless also because of the extreme license reigning in the places where it is put on, draws the curious from the four corners of the earth. The cosmopolitanism of the people who attend is notably recorded by a reporter from the *Figaro*: "The dancers...begin conversations from one end of the hall to the other; or else, overcome by giddiness, they suddenly leave their seats and begin their dance, their famous dance, that civilized Europe envies us, the dance that consists of holding the big toe of their right leg in one hand, while they jump in time to the music on the foot of their left leg. They thus turn about in one spot like dervishes, showing off a whirl of batiste underwear.... Beside me, an English couple is watching the scene.... The sturdy legs and the bloomers that are of modest dimensions or nonexistent do not frighten them. The Englishman smiles at the Pyrrhic realists; the Englishwoman gravely contemplates them through her lorgnette: 'Shocking, perhaps, but amusing, certainly.' "[41]

Such little tales are worth as much as, and sometimes more than, an illustration. In any case they help considerably to understand and make a living reality of certain illustra-

[41] Francueil, *Le Figaro,* December 1, 1890.

95. *Montmartre, Grille d'Egout.* Photograph by Henri Manuel.

96. *The Ballroom of the Moulin-Rouge.*

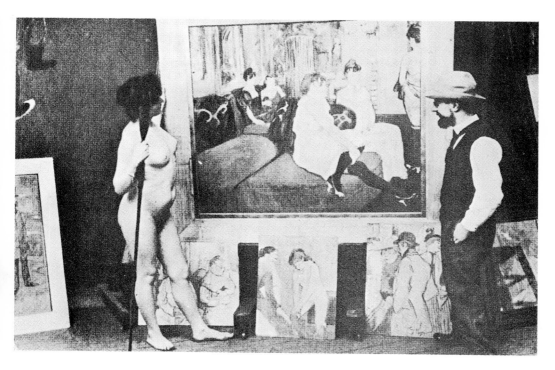

97. Photograph of Toulouse-Lautrec and a model, with some of his paintings.

98. *Movement.* Photograph. 1895. "La Lanterne Magique" Collection, Paris.

tions—photographs, drawings, and others—which we sometimes find it hard to bring to life again.

We realize when we read such eyewitness accounts that the quadrille with its companies of can-can girls and hoydens bears little relationship to what today is called a "stage show." The "dancers," who often were neither talented nor good-looking, were more like priestesses of a Carpocratian cult who go into a trance over and over again, each time setting collective desire afire in a vulgar apotheosis. Sublime and sordid—sublime *because* sordid, Lautrec would doubtless have corrected us—this rabble-rousing bacchanale perhaps has no equivalent in the recent history of public entertainment.

Frenzy

The hall, the people present, the drinks, the absinthe—everything contributes to this liturgy of the ignoble, of which a witness gives us this naturalistic glimpse:

To the infernal racket of a diabolical orchestra, the men twirl, jump, and quiver, struck with an epileptic fit; the women, their skirts raised, stick out their bellies, push their legs apart with obscene, inviting gestures, their mouths gape open in swooning grimaces; with a flick of their haunches, skirts fly, bloomers make a cracking noise, and bent in a lubricious posture, bathed in the light of the electric lamps, they smack themselves on the buttocks. And the quadrille goes on. The girls pick up a bundle of dirty laundry, gracelessly, with heavy gestures, their legs stretched taut. And the obscenity begins again, becoming more and more repellent. In the uproar of men and women spectators pressed one against the other, their hands sometimes descending and wandering, the baron's 'little skinny' looks on as a 'string-bean' opposite her embraces his dancing partner. Her wide-open eyes don't miss a single erotic gesture, which she welcomes each time with a slight puckering of her lips into a pout of

99. Illustration by Alistair for *Manon Lescaut*.

100. *Paris*. Johannes Holbek. 1898.

astonishment, of mindless depravity, and of joy at being there. She hears the conversation of tarts who offer 'anything you like for a *louis,*' the calls from one woman to another, 'I'm awfully dirty, right, Berthe?' or 'Go ahead and ask him how many times I made him in one night.'[42]

This scene takes place at the Élysée-Montmartre, on the boulevard Rochechouart, but it is repeated every evening in various establishments. At the top is the Moulin Rouge, with a more resplendent clientele, and then, more typically proletarian, come the dance halls out toward the suburbs, the Tivoli-Vauxhall, near the place de la République, whose half-faded letters on the façade can still be seen today, the Beuzon, on the rue de la Gaieté, the Progrès, on the boulevard de l'Hôpital, the Boule Blanche, on the

[42] Georges Brandimbourg, *Croquis du Vice* (Paris: Antony, 1895).

102. *Corset and bloomers.* Photograph. 1900. "La Lanterne Magique" Collection, Paris.

101. *The Strong Woman.* Matchbox cover. 1900. Luciano Emmer Collection, Rome.

boulevard d'Italie, the Parisot, on the avenue de Choisy....

In popular districts, the queens of the quadrille enjoy immense prestige, greater than that of our Brigitte Bardots and Liz Taylors. In the course of his kindly evocations of nights in Paris, Rodolphe Darzens noted this scene on a street in Montmartre: "...jealous of these pure glories, kids with their hair still down, already as perverted as their elder sisters, compete with each other, raise their leg, show off inside their lifted skirts the whitest flesh they can, darkened at

103. *Rayon d'Or, Star Dancer.* Bibliothèque Nationale, Estampes, Paris.

the groin with fuzz glimpsed momentarily."[43]

As for the young man made restless by puberty, going to see the quadrille represents his initiation into the world of men, as Jules Jouy has shown in this song:

Enfin! j'suis donc un homme complet! . . .
Du curieux livre de l'amour
La première page je l'ai lue.
Aux femmes, je m'en vais faire la cour:
J'ai vu l'pantalon d'la Goulue!

[At last I'm a real man! . . .
I've read the first page
Of the curious book of love.
I'm going to flirt with women:
I've seen La Goulue's bloomers!]

The era of underwear is also that of the leg in the air, of happiness glimpsed beneath petticoats, of frustrated desire that every obstacle sets aflame, of fleecy bypaths where Cupid lurks in the shrubbery.

It is quite natural that in these overclothed years, the occasional baring of the female body should arouse unusual interest.

With the fallacious pretext that "the nude is chaste when it is beautiful," the public at the turn of the century will find esthetic excuses to justify its appetite for the show of flesh. We shall follow this public to the theater, where the alibi of art permits boldnesses that are all the more vivacious because they answer frustrated needs.

104. *Proposed sign for a midwife.* Gerbault.

[43] Rodolphe Darzens, *Nuits à Paris* (Paris: E. Dentu, 1889).

105. *The Can-Can.* Seurat.

III.

IN FEATHERS AND BARE NAKED

Well, then don't go around
all naked.
Georges Feydeau

Pour qui votait-on? We would not have dared to make such a bad pun:* we are merely quoting it, for it served as the title of a revue at La Cigale in 1901. *Pour qui votait-on?* an announcer slyly asked. "For you, Messieurs, of course!" the cuties displaying their curves answered in chorus.

---

* Who did you vote for? A pun on *Pour qui vos tétons:* Who are your tits for? [Translator's note.]

From 1890—the approximate date that the nude ventured onstage—to 1908, which saw the birth of the "League against License in the Streets," with Senator Béranger as its president, there is a symptomatic proliferation of stage shows in which the female body is bared, partially or practically *in toto,* and comes to haunt the dreams of a whole populace that too much dallying and too many detours have starved.

From the Salon to the Theater

Operatic apotheoses, intermezzos of symbolist or realist plays, pantomimes, ballets: the nude flourishes onstage, imitating historical paintings or genre paintings shown at art exhibits. "The nude has become a part of our mores," F.-A. d'Ersky writes in 1909. "After having invaded the Salon, it necessarily had to be honored in the Theater."[44]

Things are not so simple. The nude, as a matter of fact, is accepted in the painting Salons only under certain conditions and following certain rules. The amazing scandal caused in 1863 by Manet's "Olympia," which was judged to be insolently realistic and obscene, has not been forgotten. For a long time to come, "artistic" nakedness would be accepted only if it had a halo of unreality. None of that hair on the underarm or pubis that recalls our animal nature. No scenes of

106. *The Bowler.* X. Gérôme.

---

[44] *Paris-Galant* for 1909 (Almanach littéraire et artistique, H. Daragon éditeur, Paris).

current life, which would surely turn scabrous. The nude must have a classical or heroic pretext, or the Bengal lights of fairy tales or allegory. The turn of our century could feel only horror at the cruel and lucid nudes of Degas and only uneasiness as it contemplated the sensual, undisguised flesh of Bonnard's models. Let us not forget that Jean Lorrain broke with Yvette Guilbert because she had permitted Lautrec to make her ugly.

People admire, of course, the fat sirens of Bouguereau, the naiads of Carrier-Belleuse, or the bare breast of Cormon's "Gauloise," but people of refinement nonetheless prefer the Salomes of Gustave Moreau, the Unicorns of Armand Point, and the Columbines of Jules Chéret or Alfred Willette. It is these figures who will pass, with appropriate staging, from the painter's studio to the theater.

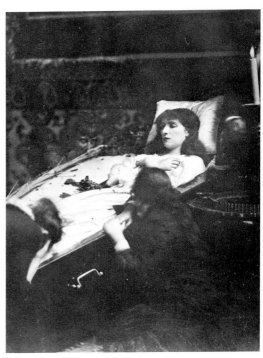

108. Sarah Bernhardt posing in the coffin she carried with her on her last tours. George Sirot Collection, Paris.

Tights and Maillots

The unveiling of the female body onstage had antecedents, but they did not go back very far. People cite, as an exception to the general rule, the example of Emma Harte in the eighteenth century; in 1780 she caused a furor in London by exhibiting herself, without veils, in the role of the goddess Hygeia. Her "mythological" dances, in which she was protected only by transparent gauze, made the most blasé dandies flock to Covent Garden. This same Emma Harte later became Lady Hamilton, Lord Nelson's mistress.

In France around 1798, a certain Maillot, a hosier for the Opera, invented a sort of fine-meshed flesh-colored knit garment which closely followed the shape of the body, and which he named after himself. Opera "tights"

107. *The Princess of Caraman-Chimay and the violinist Rigo.*

109. *A vision of plastic art.* Jean Vignes Collection, Paris.

110. *A nice round ball.* A. Penot.

were born, and were soon to have the "tutu" added to them. These two articles were the object of indignant protests and even of proposed legislative measures which were turned down.

The first appearance onstage of a nude—without cheating—apparently dates from a performance of Marlowe's *Dr. Faustus* in 1891 at the Théâtre des Arts. The bit-player playing the role of Lust in the scene of the capital sins came onstage clad in a simple drape across her haunches and a veil behind her back.[45] Francisque Sarcey, the outstanding drama critic of the period, choked with indignation, but this play, despite the fact that it was a difficult one, filled the house every night with students and young people, doubt-

less less curious about Marlowe than about the entrance onstage of the indecent Lust.

Costume Parties

In the last decade of the century there was a rash of what were called "fêtes de caractère," [character parties]. These were mostly informal dances or parties where the guests dressed up in costumes carrying out a historical theme, and where a certain freedom of costume and demeanor was permitted. Among these costume parties the most famous were the annual balls, that of the "Internat," that of the "Vache Enragée" in Montmartre, which gave rise to the "Vachalcades," that of the "Courrier Français," or that of the "Quatz-Arts," the most celebrated of all.

For this latter, apprentice painters and

[45] Dr. G.-J. Witkowsky and L. Nass, *Le Nu au Théâtre* (Paris: H. Daragon, 1909).

sculptors from the ateliers of teachers famous in that era, aided by the advice and the kindly solicitude of their patrons, unveiled masterpieces of ingenuity and imagination.

It is to be noted that the artist, once upon a time, had a vaguely suspect, equivocal reputation in the eyes of the bourgeois, owed for the most part to the simple fact that he spent his time with naked women. It took just one step further—a step that was taken, moreover—to imagine him surrounded by an erotic aura, and given to mad orgies and the worst sort of debauchery.

A vast circulation of periodicals, albums, and books supposedly for painters, marks the rise of the nude between 1890 and 1910, still protected by the magic formula: "A nude is chaste when it is beautiful." Leafing through Bayard's *Le Nu esthétique* [The Esthetic Nude], Meyer's *La Grâce féminine* [Feminine Grace], Téramond's *Les Beautés du nu* [The Beauties of the Nude], or the

111. *Dance.* Héro.

112. Design for the Fun House at the Universal Exposition. H. Gerbault. Sold at auction, 1901.

113. *The Bride*. Franz von Bayros. Illustration
for *Fleurette's Purple Snails*, first publication of
the Society of Austrian Bibliophiles.

anonymous collections placed side-by-side in book catalogues with works on flagellation, Lesbians, or houses of pleasure, one is surprised to see to what degree the theater of this period, with its living tableaux, its classical poses, its flesh-and-blood caryatids, was based on familiar themes in painting and sculpture.

The Quat-z-Arts

The Quat-z-Arts ball of 1898, whose exceptional splendor was long talked about in the gossip-columns, was theatrical, a pure example of the taste of the time. On this occasion the ateliers of Dalou, Laurens, Gérôme, and Cormon got together for a competition, with fruitful results. The cream of Paris society crowded into the Moulin Rouge to contemplate "the flabbergasting cortege," as Jean Lorrain put it. In his Pall-Mall column of April 25, 1898, the poet of *Narkiss,* the novelist of *Monsieur de Phocas* marvels: "The nudity of captives carried off on the crupper of their steeds by Cormon's Tamerlanes; the nudity of the adultress fiercely paraded in the streets of medieval cities . . . the nudity of heretics quartered on the rack; . . . there were spasms and racking of limbs, tensing of painful breasts beneath a widow's veil of disheveled hair, all the voluptuousness of suffering, tortured flesh. . . . This graceful nudity in chains among savage Huns or Grand Inquisitors was a perfect complement of the legend of the centuries."[46]

This spectacle—which was doubtless less chaste than esthetes defending it would like us to believe—is the object, despite the illustrious list of patrons who sponsored it, of severe disapproval on the part of alarmed defenders of bourgeois modesty. Among the crowd contemplating "the unforgettable pa-

114. *Singer with Feathers.* 1870. *La Vie Parisienne.*

---

[46] Jean Lorrain, *La Ville empoisonnée, Pall-Mall Paris* (Jean Crès, 1936). A posthumous collection edited by Georges Normandy.

115. *The Nude in the Theater.*

rade of sixteen Japanese, carrying the triumphant nudity of a princess of Ojeddo on a long litter, clad in nothing but the bandeaux of her heavy black hair," Jean Lorrain notes the presence of the most respectable of his contemporaries: Maurice Barrès and François Coppée, Henri Houssaye and Georges Clairin, Pierre Louÿs and Guillaume Dubufe, Georges Rochegrosse and Henry Bataille, directors of subsidized theaters who had come there to "seek inspiration, find an idea," important doctors, members of the Institute, courtesans,

young wives of artists, and even . . . yes, married women.

There are violent protests all the same, and the detractors of the Quat-z-Arts put up a desperate fight. "How illogical prejudices are!" jovial Louis Morin writes. "The mother of a family takes her daughter to the Salon, has her halt at length before the nymphs and bathers of the delightful Jules Lefebvre and the melting Bouguereau. Suppose that nymphs and bathers descend from their frames and parade their flesh of lilies and roses in the exhibition-room, and imagine the mad flight of these ladies and their cries of indignation. If the image is charming, why is the reality so detestable?"[47]

The Beautiful and the Pretty

The contrast between chaste beauty and lewd beauty upsets people in this era. In connection with this same Quat-z-Arts ball of 1898, Jean Lorrain remarks: "No obscene thoughts came to mind in the face of so much female flesh. . . . Had there been one set of tails or one modern ball gown in this crowd, the game would have been up, for the nudity of the women would have become undress and the spectacle would have become lupanarian." On the other hand, this columnist jumps at the chance to denounce the contemporary taste for what is "pretty," a term which, given the context, was probably to his mind a synonym for "salacious."

But let us not complain about this fit of moralizing which serves Jean Lorrain as a pretext for a virtuoso evocation of the most piquant aspects of spectacles in his day:

The undress of cabarets, the silky rustling underwear flung in the noses of the spectator in a froth of lace, the slyness of clocked stockings and the seductiveness of flesh-colored tights

[47] Louis Morin, *La Revue des Quat' Saisons,* No. 1, January-April, 1900, Paris, Ollendorff.

glimpsed inside black tulle bloomers are pretty; the swoop of dresses perversely slit at the hips is pretty; tense laced bosoms thrust forward in corsets that are too tight are pretty; the mystery of shoulders suddenly revealed by adroit movements of the arm, the knots of ribbon at the tops of shoulders, the raising of skirts, the vulgarity of things that gape open promisingly, and all the poetry, the vulgar, whispering, light-touched poetry of fake Louis XV fashions, provocative skirts, riotous underwear, and masquerade costumes are pretty; pretty, that's what all these things are, pretty because they are equivocal; the artful diction of Mademoiselle Guilbert, the frenzied grinds of Balthy are pretty; the enervated and enervating quivers of Marguerite Deval, as sour as a green fruit, are pretty; the way Mariette Sully, that ideal out-

116. *The Crusader and his Fiancée.* Dampt. After Maurice Rheims, *L'objet 1900,* plate 2, in color. Arts et Métiers Graphiques, 1964, Paris.

117. One of a series of drawings entitled *Liebe.* Michael von Zichy.

door-restaurant doll, acts is pretty, pretty, pretty![48]

After this mad gallop through current mores, which brings the shiver that ran down the spines of his contemporaries back to life for us, it is of little moment, it seems to us, that Jean Lorrain pretended to prefer the reconstructions of helmeted Beaux Arts Romans to the seduction of *froufrou*. Most of

---

[48] Jean Lorrain, *La Ville empoisonnée, op. cit.*

119. *Portrait of Arlette Dorgère.* Jules Chéret. 1904. Musée Jules Chéret, Nice.

118. *Parisiana Concert.* E. Rémy. Lithograph.

this is a pose on his part, and a loyalty, common to people of his time, to the nonsense about a nude being chaste when it is beautiful.

Among the ridiculous disguises parading at the Quat-z-Arts, there really must have been a few amusing or picturesque creations. But certainly what constituted the attraction of these diversions and drew such crowds to them was naked beauties: Oriental princesses, odalisques, slaves, vestals, showing off their haunches and their breasts, tempting visions, prudently described as chaste...by hypocrites, though many a spectator would take home lascivious memories of them.

Classical Spectaculars

Heroines of historical tableaux, springing completely armed from the bold composi-

120. Mademoiselle Lidia's striptease act on a trapeze at the Olympia. *Le Panorama, op. cit.*

tions of the Laurenses or the Moreaus, will be queens of the stage for several years.

All antiquity will serve to dress—and more often still to undress—the modern priestesses of Terpsichore. (Please pardon us if the style of the time occasionally gets the better of us.) Tanagra vases, which are all the rage, will come to life through the gracefulness of Isadora Duncan with her body of a callipygian goddess. Salome, after Aubrey Beardsley and Oscar Wilde, will inspire Maud Allan and Mademoiselle Cerutti. *Paris-Galant* publishes the picture—too badly printed to be able to reproduce it here, unfortunately—of a Mademoiselle Pépée, her lovely bosom set with precious stones and gold, whose Egyptian dances promised to be gorgeous esthetic outpourings. She had a rival, Mademoiselle Isis, who seems to have been better than she was. F.-A. d'Ersky says of this latter: "In her ritual dances of an-

cient Egypt, especially those of the 'Veil' and the 'Lotus,' in her celebration of the 'Mysteries of Isis,' this delicate bare-breasted dancer is truly admirable."[49]

It was rather common—we do not know for certain, however, whether it was a question of a commercial come-on or a desire to create "atmosphere"—for plays to be embellished by intermezzos with naked dancers. In 1906 at the Comédie Royale, Mademoiselle Myrtis, we are told, "was acclaimed when she performed a ravishing serpent dance, in the course of Monsieur Nozière's strange play, *L'Après-midi byzantine* [The Byzantine Afternoon]. Mysterious and sweet, with her smile that is so naturally ingenuous, the little dancer drew you toward love and death."[50]

[49] *Paris-Galant*, 1909.
[50] F.-A. d'Ersky, "Le Nu sur la Scène," in *Paris-Galant* for 1909, Paris, H. Daragon.

121. *End-of-the-year-Revue.* A. Guillaume.

Theaters with a reputation for seriousness unhesitatingly have recourse to this much-appreciated added ingredient, the naked dancer. Jean Lorrain, who sees everything, devotes his Pall-Mall column of December 10, 1895, to a Hindu play by Kalidasa, *L'Anneau de Cakuntala* [The Ring of Cakuntala], adapted by Ferdinand Hérold and performed at the Théâtre de l'Oeuvre. "Where," Lorrain writes, "does Monsieur Lugné-Poe get the little women or rather the little virgins that he presents us with, delightfully nude and chaste, in Hindu or Norwegian plays on which he has a monopoly?"[51] And the columnist describes the disturbing sacred virgins for us: "Nayva with her frail, supple arms, her young torso sheathed in a simple drapery, and a calm, delicate oval face framed in black hair... Mademoiselle Béraldi, [who] recalls Leonardo's women, while the other, Mademoiselle Auclair, with a tormented profile and a firm chin beneath

51 Jean Lorrain, *Poussières de Paris, op. cit.*

122. *The Lady Animal Trainer.* Toulouse-Lautrec.

a thick blonde fleece of hair, calls to mind one of Gozzoli's androgynous angels...."

This same Théâtre de l'Oeuvre, emancipated only a short time before, was the scene of the first performance of a dramatic poem by Charles Van Lerbergue, *Le Grand Pan* [The Great Pan], under the direction, as usual, of Lugné-Poe. Colette's charm was a complete contrast to what was customarily called beauty in her day: thin, supple, nervous, sharp-faced, she played the young virgin victim of the god Pan in this play. She was dressed in rags; her tattered, torn dress stopped at the middle of her upper leg, baring her thighs, as wiry as a nanny goat's, and she wore no tights under these rags. "Her fiery dance before the cortege of the God evoked images of ancient bacchanales," Nozières wrote in *Le Matin*.

The public gradually became accustomed

123. *Sarah Brown.* Photograph by Ogereau. *Le Panorama, op. cit.*

124. Rita Marck (of La Scala, Paris) at the costume ball of the Countess d'Urville.

to finding the unclad intermezzo that warmed its heart in plays of all sorts. When Henry Bataille's *La Femme Nue* [The Naked Woman] was given, this public was sorely disappointed, because it was left hungry despite the provocative title. On the other hand, François de Curel's *La Fille Sauvage* [The Wild Girl] played to full houses, less by reason of the grandiloquent dialogue of the noble author of the *Fossiles* [Fossils] than by virtue of the presence of Suzanne Després,

126. *The Way Girls Dance.* Pézilla. 1903. *Froufrou.*

who performed her role entirely naked beneath a snuff-colored extra-tight maillot.

Pantomimes and Living Tableaux

Numerous authors—whose reputations are not always bad—compose sketches and pantomimes which have no other purpose than to bring nudes before the public eye. The Cirque Molier seems to have specialized in undress in the nineties. As early as 1888, Félieien Champsaur gave a pantomime entitled *Les Éreintés de la Vie* [Those Beaten by Life] there, the plot of which was quite monumentally stupid but which allowed the introduction of naked women walking with crutches or dragging about with other more or less conspicuous infirmities.

The same Cirque Molier in 1891 mounts a grand pantomime-spectacle, *Sardanapale*

125. *Anna Held.*

127. *Zina de Riska.* Photograph by Berthaud. *Le Panorama, op. cit.*

et du Falzar.* It is about a fake doctor who has founded a hydrotherapy establishment whose walls have peekholes for voyeurs. Thus panels open and the audience can admire superb bare-breasted creatures in the bathtub or shower. Simple, isn't it?

At the Folies-Bergère, at the Moulin

---

* *The Games of Love and a Pair of Pants.* This is a parody of the title of a famous play by Marivaux: *Le Jeu de l'amour et du hasard: The Game of Love and Chance.* [Translator's note.]

128. *Mademoiselle d'Yliac.* Photograph by Walery.

[Sardanapalus], in which the curtain rises on a voluptuous group of young girls clad only in their jewels. "A splendid apotheosis of pink and white flesh," the program announces.

But it is the Divan Japonais that enjoys the greatest success between 1894 and 1897, thanks to pantomimes whose object is clearly set forth in the titles: *Le Coucher d'Yvette* [Yvette's Retirement for the Night], *Le Bain de Liane* [Liane's Bath], *Bains de Dames* [Ladies' Baths], *Suzanne au Bain* [Suzanne in Her Bath], *Emilienne aux Quat-z-Arts* [Emilienne at the Quat-z-Arts Ball]. Suzanne Derval and Bob Walter, who was so tiny that Jean Lorrain nicknamed her "Bob Parterre" [Bob Seat-Downstairs], shone in these exhibitions justified by the thinnest of plots.

The genre spread and reached the little theaters, as this poster title from La Cigale in 1903 bears witness: *Les Jeux de l'amour*

91

Rouge, at the Olympia, at the Variétés, at Bobino, people prefer living tableaux, inspired by the masterpieces of academic art. Costly reproductions of Thomas Couture's "La Décadence Romaine" [Roman Decadence] or of Ingres's "Le Bain turc" [The Turkish Bath] are mounted. This tradition has been perpetuated and still flowers at Monsieur Henri Varna's Casino de Paris, and at Monsieur Paul Derval's Folies-Bergère.

As an index of the taste of the time, we came across this interesting invitation card from the year 1906:

The Director of Pigall's Restaurant requests the honor of X's presence at the *strictly private* exceptional Artistic Evening of Living

129. Mesdemoiselles Myrtis of the Alhambra [at right] and de Courcelles [below].

Tableaux and Greek Dances that it will offer in its Salons, 11, place Pigall, on Tuesday March third.

This Evening will be preceded by a Dinner which will be served promptly at eight-thirty, at a price of twenty francs per person (wine not included) and followed by a beauty contest with a battle of flowers.

R.S.V.P., indicating the number of places reserved.

Dominos and costumes are recommended.

By a very natural process whereby one bid tops another, the nude in the theater became, especially after 1900, more and more suggestive, and even lewd, to such a point that public authorities in 1907 grew alarmed, and at the instigation of leagues and associations protecting "the family" and "public morals" there broke out what has been called "the war of the nude."

We have noticed the suggestive title of a

revue at La Cigale: *Pour qui votait-on?* This perfect double-entendre is far from being the only one. *Qui complote? Paris complote,** or *Y a des Fez!*† reflect a spirit which glitters, in literature, all through the works of Willy.

Moreover, between 1899 and 1908 there are more and more theaters devoted exclusively to the exhibition of nudes, as is demonstrated by these titles: *Nue Cocotte* [The Naked Tart], *As-tu vu mon nu?* [Have You Seen My Nude?], *Tout à l'oeil...nu* [All with the Naked...Eye],** *Paris sans fil* [Wireless Paris], *Nichonette* [The Girl with the Little Tits], *J'veux du nu, na* [I Want Some Nudes, So There], *Dénichons* [Let's Fly from the Nest],‡ put up out front one after the other by Les Ambassadeurs, La Cigale, La Fourmi, Ba-Ta-Clan, La Gaieté Montparnasse, and La Scala, along with other theaters that have long since disappeared. The only trace today of this pleasantly naughty tradition is the Concert Mayol, managed by the excellent Lucien Rimmels, who also makes up the reviews and writes their racy book.

These little theaters reserved for gallant spectacles were no longer content with living tableaux and classical scenes. To judge from reports, directors, costume designers, and authors no longer went about things in a gingerly way. Here, for example, is what Armande Cassive, in a costume that went beyond décolleté, sang in *Loute*, by Pierre Veber, at the Capucines in 1902:

A qui c'est, mon chat-chat,
Ces deux p'tits vagabonds-là?
    C'est à toi
    Mon beau roi,
Ces nichons ça t'appartient
Embrass' les, embrass' les bien,
C'est à toi mon gros chien-chien!

[Who, my kitty-cat,
  Do these two little vagabonds belong to?
    They're yours,
    My handsome king,
  These boobs belong to you
  Kiss them, kiss them nicely,
  They're yours, my doggy dear!]

Cassive was nonetheless a queen of the day, fêted in the Bois and at Maxim's, where

130. *The Jewel.*

---

* Who's plotting? Paris is plotting. A pun on *Qui qu'on pelote? Paris qu'on pelote:* Who's getting felt up? Paris is. [Translator's note.]

† Fezzes here! A pun on: *Y a des fesses:* Buttocks here! [Translator's note.]

** Also a pun on *Tout à l'oeil:* Everything free! [Translator's note.]

‡ Also a pun on *Des nichons:* Tits. [Translator's note.]

131. *Actress Suzanne Desprès.*

she appeared on the arm of Maurice Donnay, who was soon to be elected to the French Academy.

Suggestive Double Meanings

Erotic suggestion is the indispensable leavening in every good repertory. Yvette Guilbert's songs are equivocal, deliberately full of double meanings. Polin sang—exquisitely, it appears—verses full of double-entendres, which the following refrain gives us some idea of:

> Ah! Mad'moiselle Rose,
> J'ai un p'tit objet,
> Un p'tit objet
> À vous offrir.
> Oui, j'ai quelque chose
> Qui vous f'ra plaisir!

> [Ah! Mademoiselle Rose,
> I have a little something,
> A little something
> To offer you
> Yes, I have something
> That will please you!]

And Dranem, who sang standing in pro-file with his eyes closed—a detail that so impressed Arletty that she still marvels at it—proceeded for thirty insane verses or so with this ambiguous refrain:

> J'l'ai trempée dans l'amidon:
> C'est un excellent remède.
> Comm' ça ell' est restée raide
> Pendant huit jours environ.

> [I soaked it in starch
> That's an excellent remedy.
> So it stayed stiff
> For about a week.]

Among the transcriptions of the librettos of revues or songs from the beginning of the century, we found some which are perhaps extreme cases, but which seemed to us so surprising that we cannot refrain from citing them here.

We shall cite in particular a scene from the revue *Tu l'as l'Cri-cri* [You've Caught the Cricket], presented at the Gaieté-Rochechouart in 1907. Young women dressed as farmerettes—but in such a way that their charms were visible—form a circle around one of their number who comes upstage and sings:

94

132. *Anna Held.* Photograph by Reutlinger. *Le Panorama, op. cit.*

Quand on veut traire gentiment
    Gracieusement
Il faut avoir la main douce
    Et sans secousse . . .
Délicatement on agite,
    Pas trop vite,
Et dès qu'on sent que le lait
    A jaillir va être prèt,
On dirige droit le jet
    Avec prudence.

[When you want to milk nicely,
    Gracefully,
  You must have gentle hands
    That aren't rough . . .
  You go about it delicately
    Not too fast
  And when you feel that the milk
    Is ready to spurt out,
  You aim the stream straight
    Carefully.]

THE FARM GIRLS:
    Ffft! Ffft! Ffft!

FIRST FARM GIRL:
    Ffft! Ffft! Ffft!

FARM GIRLS:
    Ffft! Ffft! Ffft!

These *ffft*s must have made the spectator pant. But there is better yet to come. At the Parisiana, in 1906, the revue *Viens-tu chéri?* [Are You Coming, Dearie?] was enhanced by a scene played by two ravishing young actresses, one of them in the mere pretense of a cat costume and the other, just as thinly clad, displaying the attributes of the tongue. And this is the duet they sang:

Oui, voici, sans faire de harangue,
Le p'tit Chat et son amie la Langue.
Nous aimons le léger badinage
Et tous deux nous faisons bon ménage.
Mais ce soir, pour qu' la fêt' soit complète,
Nous allons devant vous faire . . . causette!

[Yes, here, without preaching
  Are the Little Cat and his friend the Tongue.
  And the two of us get along nicely together.
  But tonight, for the party to be complete,
  We're going to . . . have a little chat in front
    of you.]

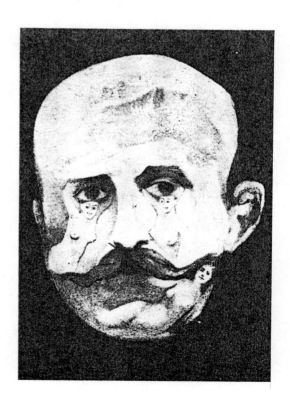

133. *Caillaux.* Photo-montage.

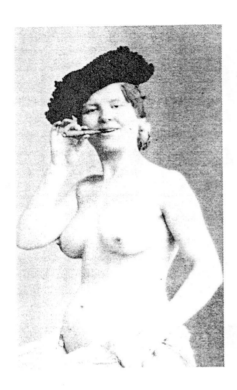

134. *Love at the Bullfight.* 1895.

136. *The Martinis,* the naked skaters at the rink.

135. *Suzanne Desprès,* on an ashtray. *Le Pano-rama, op. cit.*

So far as we know, these ribaldries got across the footlights without provoking troublesome comment. Sometimes—rarely, however—some censor or other took offense.

Scandals

Lafargue's *La Revue à Poivre* [The Pepper Revue] at La Scala in 1903 apparently went beyond the limits of what was allowable.

137. *Proh* [sic] *Pudor.* Homage to the League
against License in the Streets. A. Rouveyre.

Mademoiselle Taxil enjoyed great personal
success in it, thanks to a state of undress that
was pervertedly refined. In the beginning,
Mademoiselle Taxil's right breast was absolutely bare: a jeweled patch, fastened to a
stem at the edge of her bodice, covered only
her nipple, which was represented by a large
diamond surrounded by an aureole of diamonds. Among other songs, Mademoiselle
Taxil sang:

Femm', femm', femm',
C'est not' réclame
Ces p'tits monts où l'on s'pâme,
Les jeunes cornichons
Et les vieux cochons
En pincent pour nos nichons!

[Women, women, women,
That's the bargain we're advertising
Those little mountains you swoon on,
Young imbeciles
And old pigs
Have a crush on our boobs!]

138. *Mademoiselle Blanche-de-Neige.* Photograph by Reutlinger.

139. *Boska and Darbel,* "captains" of the revue at the Folies-Bergère, 1911.

A journalist indignantly leaped on his pen: "It's not pepper; it's ginger, cubeb, Spanish fly!" And to further justify his disapproval, he gives us a valuable description of this *Revue à Poivre*: "At certain moments, this lewd furor, this frenzy, go so far that embarrassment and uneasiness spread through the hall. An example: Monsieur Lafargue brings onstage several young people in an extreme state of undress, but the sight of them does not offend us because for the most part they are pretty and have nice figures. Each one of them symbolizes a part of a woman's body: one of them the back, another the bosom, another the stomach, another the thighs, another . . . please do not make me finish the list. A person whose elegant title in the program is "Coordinator of the Parts" comes onstage. I shall not describe the dialogue in detail; it gives off a smell of such vulgar animality that more than one auditor was secretly nauseated."[52]

Provocative obscenity becomes even more direct in 1906 at the Gaieté-Montparnasse, where baker-women appear wearing caps in the form of little split rolls resembling the female genitals. Conversely, at the Concert de la Pépinière, the phallus appears onstage in the form of a goldbeater's-skin condom that an announcer elegantly blows up. It

[52] Dr. A.-J. Witkowsky and L. Nass: *Le Nu au Théâtre* (Paris: H. Daragon, 1909).

seems as if one is in the mad world of Clovis Trouille, and it is very possible that this peculiarly inspired painter of the "Palais des Mirages" [Palace of Mirages] and "Oh Calcutta," who was acquainted with this facet of life in Paris in his youth, was able to get out of it, as a poet termed it, "provisions to last a long time."

The Little-Palace

Libertine boldness, however, reached its climax in 1908 under Monsieur de Chatillon, the director of the Little-Palace, who presented an extremely spicy pantomime called *Griserie d'Éther* [Ether-Intoxication]. This drop—of ether—that makes the cup run over unleashed a press campaign, led by *L'Autorité*, and a string of lawsuits as well. Jules Delahaye, a deputy from Maine-et-Loire, sent a bailiff to the theater and he drew up an affidavit. The "Little-Palace affair," brought before the bar of justice, gave rise to a court decree, the most important sections of which read as follows:

In view of the fact that in the course of this pantomime Mesdemoiselles Bouzon and Lepelley acted out a drunken scene with Lesbian passions, and that Mademoiselle Lepelley leans back in an armchair, baring her torso and her breasts, whereas Mademoiselle Bouzon sits down next to her, and baring her breasts and torso also, presses up against her, and takes her in her arms, placing her mouth on hers, caressing her breasts with her hand, which she also allowed to wander lower;

That the embrace ended only so as to permit Mademoiselle Lepelley to express, through the motions displayed on her physiognomy and the quivering of her body, the erotic excitement provoked by the caresses of which she had just been the object;

That at the end of this scene and after these contacts Mademoiselle Bouzon stood up, her chemise having fallen below her knees, and

140. *Love and Duty.* Philippe Heyl. 1901 Salon.

141. *The Lustful Donkey.* Photo-montage. 1900.

99

142. *The Beautiful Female Faun.* H. Gerbault. 1900. *La Vie Parisienne.*

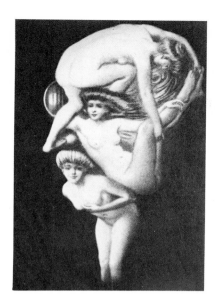

143. *An old rake* in the style of Archimboldo. Postcard. 1900.

144. *The Faun.* Photo-montage in the style of Archimboldo. 1900.

seized a bouquet of roses that she placed before her private parts;

In view of the fact that such a nude exhibition, accompanied by these embraces, these poses, these caresses, these kisses or their simulacrum, and intended only to serve as a display of nervous passions, can be considered only as an appeal to the most vulgar, the most disturbing, and the most dangerous lewdness. . . .

Monsieur de Chatillon was condemned to three months in prison in all and fined two hundred francs, whereas Mesdemoiselles Bouzon and Lepelley were given a suspended sentence of one month and fined fifty francs.

The War of the Nude

Excess of any sort is damaging and the general offensive conducted by Senator Bèranger against the nude in the theater was, in the long run, a failure. The fact is that, judging from hearsay rather than from his own experience, this respectable Conscript Father thoughtlessly censored spectacles that his contemporaries did not consider shocking at all. The Folies-Royales, especially, was still at the stage of presenting living tableaux in which the treasures of the Salons came to life on the stage. Mesdemoiselles Berthe Laisney, Aimée Thierry, and Suzanne Duhaut incarnated the figures in these celebrated works: the *Femme au Masque* [Woman with the Mask], *L'Amour et Psyché* [Love and Psyche], and *Les Trois Grâces* [The Three Graces]. Though it is true that these handsome creatures displayed themselves nude, they at least were immobile, depilated, and provided with panties: they were, in a word, chaste.

At the Folie-Pigalle, which was also haled into court by the forces of modesty, Made-

145. Study for Verlaine's *Parallèlement*. Pierre
Bonnard. Sketch in blue crayon. 1900. Robert
Lebel Collection, Paris.

146. *The Palace of Marvels (Homage to Art Nouveau)*. Clovis Trouville.

moiselle Germaine Aymos played in *Dans un Rêve* [In a Dream], a pantomime by Chassigneux, with music by Esteban-Marti. A sculptor, lonely and overcome with sadness, seeks inspiration, when suddenly Myrto (Mademoiselle Aymos) appears through the clouds, raising her veils, naked as Phryne except for a pearl necklace around her neck and a jeweled girdle about her waist.

Various personalities belonging to the world of journalism, letters, arts, and the theater, among them Jules Claretie, André Antoine, Pierre Louÿs, Sarah Bernhardt, Lise Fleuron, Ernest Lajeunesse, Pedro Gailhard, the former director of the Opera, and Georges Normandy, vigorously defended the Folies-Royales and the Folie-Pigalle, and their directors were acquitted.

The Nude Wins Out

It must be noted that the somewhat hypocritical zeal of the assailers of the nude was not shared by any large number of people. There is reason to believe that habit blunts indignation. Old Uncle Francisque Sarcey, whom we have seen blushing at Marlowe's *Dr. Faustus* in 1891, in which Lust displayed herself naked, seems to have calmed down considerably over the years. He is not displeased when he attends the *Revue Chaste* at the Divan Japonais in 1899, in which there is

147. *Colette at the Ba-Ta-Clan.*

a splendid duel between blonde Lise Dérieux and brunette Cyclamen Daix, which he reports on in his drama-column in the *Temps*: "Both of them take off their clothes, or rather their bodices; all that remains is a chemisette which falls in the heat of action; each of them faces her opponent's fencing foil with a perfectly bare bosom. Mademoiselle Cyclamen Daix is young and very pretty, and sings nicely. Mademoiselle Dérieux would have the first prize for bosoms *ex aequo*; she would win only second prize for all the rest."

The female nude, a source of scandal at the beginning, in the end took twenty years to win a place on the stage. Despite certain

149. *Ceres*. Photographic composition. 1898.

148. *Réjane*. Photograph by Reutlinger.

abuses, which were censored now and then, it won out over puritan offensives and took its place in the mores of the time. To really understand the extraordinary attraction it had at the time, one must imagine oneself back in that stilted, formalist, strait-laced era, whose barriers tumble one by one. However naïve, and even comical, these spectacles that intoxicated our predecessors may seem at times today, we must picture what a liberating safety-valve they were for them. With things thus put in their proper perspective, we shall perhaps be inclined not so much to poke fun at their ridiculousness as to be moved by their candor.

150. *Mother and Daughter*. Edgar Chahine. Crayon. 1893.

IV.

GREEN FRUITS

We are not exactly leaving the domain of
the theater when we point, in the firmament
of Eros 1900, to the passage of a comet with
a delicate and sinuous tail, with hair tied
back by a schoolgirl's ribbon, and bearing the
name of Claudine.

Claudines

A savory tetralogy with the sharp taste of
English cherries and ginger, the *Claudine*
books, published one right on the heels of
the other from 1900 to 1903, brought considerable, though passing, glory to a versatile
writer who was already very well known:
Henry Gauthier-Villars, better known under
the pen name of Willy.[53]

We have long known that the *Claudine*
books were not, for the most part, the work
of Gauthier-Villars, but rather of his young
wife Colette. Willy contributed, it seems,
only a little retouching and a few additions,
among them puns, for he was the uncon-
tested master-punster of Paris. When their

---

[53] Willy: *Claudine à l'École,* cover illustrated
by E. della Suda (Paris: Ollendorff, 1900);
Claudine à Paris, cover illustrated by Rassenfosse
(Paris: Ollendorff, 1901); *Claudine en Ménage*
(Paris: Société du "Mercure de France," 1902);
Claudine s'en va, cover illustrated by E. Pascaud
(Paris: Ollendorff, 1903). Later editions are
signed both Willy and Colette Willy. [*Claudine
at School,* the first of the series, was first published in English in 1930 by A. and C. Boni,
New York. A more recent translation was published by Farrar, Straus & Giroux, New York,
in 1957.]

151. *Slender Nymphet.* A. Rouveyre.

152. *Dodo at Thirteen Years of Age.* Photograph from an album used in a Paris bordello, early 1900's.

Claudine and Lolita

Who was Claudine? A little girl. Today we would say a "nymphet," for Vladimir Nabokov popularized the term in his novel *Lolita.* Though sixty years separate them, and though account must be taken of their differences, the smashing success of both *Claudine* and *Lolita* stems from an exploitation of the same emotion: the troubled feelings that immature young girls, or girls in the toils of puberty, inspire in many men past forty. In Colette, it is the little girl who speaks, describing her impatience and her curiosity, the play of sensual hands, overintimate friendships, mingling—with an art that is not without its share of trickery—real memories and true-to-life description with suggestive confabulations that do no more than brush the reader lightly, the images of them vanishing before the reader at a certain point as the cape of the matador vanishes before

entente came to an end, Colette claimed the authorship that rightly belonged to her and pursued, by herself, a very successful career in literature. Her name still shines brightly, and a number of her writings are classics, whereas Willy, now almost forgotten, is hardly read except by confirmed collectors.

It is probable, however, that without Willy there would have been no *Claudine* books. Colette wrote them, at his order, when she was twenty-six. When Willy saw the first manuscript of *Claudine à l'École* [Claudine at School], he did not think much of it. Then he changed his mind, put it into shape, published it, publicized it, took all the credit for it, made it his property, identified himself with the male hero, made Colette wear the costume of her schoolgirl and behave like her, and did so much so well, in fact, that with the increasing success of the book the couple, a living advertisement, became the cynosure of all eyes.

153. *Claudine at School.* Loysel. Bronze. Circa 1904. Dorothea Tanning Collection, Paris.

154. *Little Girl.* Pierre Bonnard. 1893. Annette Vaillant Collection, Paris.

the muzzle of the bull. Nabokov, conversely, relates the fears, the worries, the torments, and the delights of a forty-year-old man cowed by a little twelve-year-old girl. We are not trying in the least to draw parallels between these two books, completely different in conception and written on completely different levels, but we think it useful to emphasize the fact that the two books attracted an immense readership for one and the same reason: the public's erotic interest in little girls or adolescent girls.

Infallible signs attest to the unheard-of popularity of Claudine. No sooner had *Claudine en Ménage* [Claudine Sets Up Housekeeping], the third volume in the series, made its appearance than Paris was inundated with advertisements for such products as Claudine lotion (prepared by Boyer,

108, avenue de Paris, La Plaine Saint-Denis, Seine); Claudine ice cream, at Latinville's, a Paris ice-cream parlor; Claudine perfume, prepared by Théric, a perfumer in Marseilles (Bouches-du-Rhône); the Claudinet, a turn-down collar and bias-striped cravat for women and children, advertised in the catalogue of La Samaritaine department store in April, 1903; a Claudine hat, at Lewis's, rue Saint-Honoré, Paris; Willy rice powder (clinging and invisible); plus a Claudine lotion, Claudine cigarettes, and even Claudine photographic plates and paper bearing no indication of where they came from.

Striking while the iron was hot, Willy began in 1902 to adapt Colette's novels for the theater, beginning with *Claudine à Paris* [Claudine in Paris], a three-act comedy, preceded by a one-act prologue: *Claudine à*

155. *Colette*. Photograph by Reutlinger.

156. *Willy.* After *Willy, En bombe,* Milsson, Paris, n.d. [1904?].

l'École, both signed Willy and Luvay (Luvay was the collective pseudonym of Lugné-Poe and Charles Vayre). The two successes—that of the novel and that of the play—reinforced each other, and the haunting image of Claudine was to be around for a long time.

Polaire

We must associate with this triumph that of the person who played Claudine onstage, Émilie-Marie Bouchaud, better known as Polaire. It was a stroke of genius, undoubtedly, for Willy to have sought out an actress of a special type to play his schoolgirl, an actress who overnight brought pleasure-seeking Paris a new sort of thrill as she proceeded from the Européen to the Eldorado and then to La Scala.

Polaire! This was the fine name chosen by this future star who had cherished one dream since childhood: to set the stage afire. This *"pied noir,"* that is, a European born in Algeria, was born in the city of Rovigo and grew up in Algiers, where she picked up the accent of Bab-el-Oued, which she kept and which made her singing all the more charming.

She was thirteen when she came, all by herself, to Paris to join her brother Edmond, who was just beginning to acquire a solid reputation as a comedian in the little theaters, under the name of Dufleuve. We know, through various witnesses, that this Dufleuve was a real professional and had a genuine gift for comedy, though his repertory was so obscene that it would be unacceptable today. We have rediscovered the lyrics he himself composed for one of his successes of 1904— he was at this time billed as a star—entitled "Mettez-y un doigt" [Put a Finger In It]. This was the chorus:

> Mettez-y un doigt
> Et puis vous verrez.
> Vous en mettrez un, après, ça deux, après ça
> trois,
> Quand on y a goûté,
> C'est la vérité,
> On veut r'commencer
> Et y a plus moyen d' s'en passer.

> [Put a finger in it
> And you'll see.
> You'll put one in, then two, and then three,
> When you've tried it
> It's true
> You want to start over again
> And you can't do without it.]

Little Émilie-Marie, who was not yet Polaire, went to see Dufleuve rehearsing at the

157. *Willy and a "fake Colette," En bombe, op. cit.*

Européen and was so impatient that one day, able to bear it no longer, she learned a song and presented herself at an audition. Her song "De la flûte au trombone" [From the Flute to the Trombone], a little insanity in the taste of the time having no other purpose than to be a vehicle for risqué allusions, with a chorus frequently interrupted with *Dzim boum boums* and *Trou-la-las*, was belted out with so much fire and, no doubt, such appealing awkwardness, that the postulant was hired on the spot. She took the name Polaire; she was fourteen years old.

It is understandable why we accord a privileged place to this child-star whose lissomeness, surprising seductiveness, and high sexual tension had the power to turn minds toward a new erotic pole.

Madame Landolf, the costume designer

who in 1900 was what Madame Rasimi was in the twenties, turned her clever hand to making Polaire's very personal stage costumes, which Colette remembered for a long time: "A dress for a paper-doll, with little graduated flounces in iridescent blue and green taffeta. . . . A dress the color of Polaire's skin, with a Prairie Indian's diadem, in violet. . . . A mulatto's dress, snow-white, whipped up to a froth. . . . A dress with a rainbow beneath the skirt, wrapped around two thin, black, firm, silk-clad legs, of an exotic elegance and agility."[54]

Not at all astonished by this extraordinary leap from the shadows, Polaire in a few months passes from curtain-raisers at the Européen to top billing at La Scala, which

---

[54] Colette, *Mes apprentissages, op. cit.*

for singers is more or less what the Comédie Française is for actors. She has a lower-class public, which stamps its feet in rhythm to acclaim her, and at the same time she attracts dandies, men of elegance, the most blasé of night-prowlers.

Her repertory, as the genre requires, leans heavily on the equivocal, on erotic double-entendres in a comic setting:

> Hildebrandt, Hildebrandt,
> Comme t'es excitant!
> Tu joues toujours dans le vif!
> Ah! r'dis-moi ton motif!

> [Hildebrandt, Hildebrandt,
> How exciting you are!
> You always play it up to the hilt!
> Tell me again what you're up to!]

Or there is this "Portrait du petit chat" [Portrait of the Little Cat] which gave rise to suggestive mimicry:

> Allons, mon p'tit matou,
> Viens vite, dis-moi tout,
> Pas Possible?... Vraiment?
> Parole?... Ah! C'est charmant!

> [Come, come, my little tomcat
> Come quick and tell me everything,
> You can't?... Really?
> Your word of honor?... Oh, that's
>   charming!]

(then, turning to the audience):

> Si vous voulez surprendre
> C'que sa pudeur cacha
> Faudrait, pour mieux m'comprendre,
> Donner vot' langue au chat!

158. *Little Brother's Soldiers* from *La Grenouilliers,* portfolio with fifteen drawings by Choisy le Conin (Franz von Bayros).

[If you want to surprise
What his modesty is concealing
To get my point, you'd have to
Give up guessing altogether*!]

Colette tells us that "as Polaire sang this undistinguished material, she tensed her whole body, shivering like a wasp caught in glue, her mouth smiling convulsively as if she had just drunk the juice of a green lemon."[55]

Golden Cantharides

To describe the birth of this star—whose splendor is already causing many a glory to pale by comparison, this living battery whose mere presence electrifies—contemporaries, at a loss for words, murmured "frenzy," "hysteria." In his column begun not long before,

* Literally, "give your tongue to the cat." [Translator's note.]
[55] *Ibid.*

160. *Les Cousines de la Colonel.* Detail from a drawing by Félicien Rops.

...dine at School.

which he writes with amused nonchalance, sensitive Jean de Tinan, visibly disturbed, speaks of the "unreal, adorable, and hateful Polaire."[56]

But it is in rereading Jean Lorrain that we find, as usual, the most vivid image of the girl he calls "golden cantharides":

As you know, she's a little slip of a girl, with a painfully thin waist, agonizingly thin, so thin it almost breaks, in a bodice so tight it gives her spasms, the prettiest sort of thinness! and in the aureole of an ultrafashionable grand lady's extravagant hat, an orange hat with a plume of iris leaves, her large voracious mouth, her immense black eyes with bruised blue circles beneath them, her incandescent pupils, the phosphorus, sulfur, and red pepper of this face

[56] *Mercure de France,* February, 1898.

of a ghoul and of Salome—all this is the exciting, the excited Polaire!

But that is nothing. What diabolical mimicry, what coffee-mill twirling of her legs, and what a belly dance! With her yellow skirts tucked up, sheathed in clocked stockings, Polaire skips about, trembles, quivers, dances with her hips, her lower back, and her navel, mimes every sort of tremor, twists, thrusts her bosom out, twists her . . . shows the whites of her eyes, miaows, swoons, and . . . vanishes . . . and to what music and what words!

The audience, frozen with amazement, forgets to applaud.[57]

Despite the ovations she got every night, Polaire dreamed of being an actress. Cheekily, brazenly, she introduced herself one day to the great director Antoine, whom she intoxicated with the story of her life, seeking to persuade him to hire her. Antoine did not frequent music halls and had never seen Polaire. Without being able to get a word in edgewise, he underwent this voluble onslaught, then got up and said to her: "Do you know you're terrifying? You positively terrify me!"[58]

The Haunting Schoolgirl

One can thus imagine how joyously Polaire welcomed Willy when he came to offer her the role of Claudine. She was eighteen at the time. What Polaire did with the role, all witnesses agree, was unforgettable. And the image of the schoolgirl with her short hair, her white collar with a large bow, her black apron with a plaid skirt showing underneath, possessed crowds of people like a sly obsession.

A man who knew what he was up to when it came to advertising stunts, Willy im-

[57] Jean Lorrain, *La Ville empoisonnée, op. cit.*
[58] *Polaire par elle-même* (Paris: Eugène Figuière, n.d.)

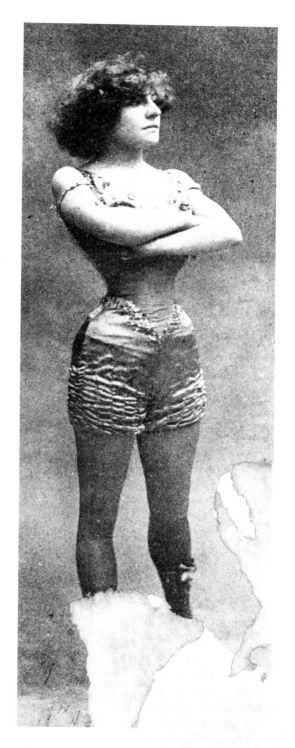

161. Polaire in *L   i* Berger.

mediately conceived the idea of a living poster. He got Colette to cut her hair short like Polaire's, made the two of them dress in identical tailored suits, pinched in at the waist and short-skirted, and paraded about, flanked by these ambiguous tomboy twins, letting people believe the rumor that the three of them lived together in a *ménage à trois* that popular imagination immediately credited with Babylonian morals.

Polaire was assailed by letters asking favors, pleas for help, enflamed missives: provincial squires, old bachelors, schoolboys with bees in their bonnet, Lesbians of all sorts, bawds—she "polarized," we might say, a prodigious outpouring of desire, spurred on by the promise of forbidden delights.

"Claudine was the height of fashion; the ambition of all the traffickers in love was to procure her . . . so, upon my soul, they simply launched ersatz Claudines! Nightclubs, elegant call-houses, and even the most miserable brothel, all had their "Claudine," in a black smock with a large white collar and a big red bow, and, of course, short hair."[59]

When Willy—with his potbelly, his walrus mustache, his bald forehead bulging out beneath a flat-brimmed top hat, and his shirt front hidden by a monumental bow—made his entrance at the Ice Palace (one of the favorite haunts of the cream of Paris society) with his feline "twins," one on each arm, a silence greeted them, followed by a prolonged murmur. Jean Cocteau, who at this time was still very young, also frequented this fashionable skating rink, where he saw Sem, a "fierce insect," armed with his Koh-I-Nor crayon, not far from "a thin, thin Colette; a sort of little fox in a cycling costume, a sort of fox-terrier in skirts, with a black patch over her eye, fastened to her temple with a bow of red ribbon."

Cocteau liked to stay late, watching for the arrival of artists and cocottes. "Then," he writes, "there suddenly appeared a creature whose name in these precincts was already a masterpiece: Polaire! With a flat yellow serpent's head balancing the Portuguese oysters of her eyes with the gleam of mother-of-pearl and salt and cool shadow, her features strained, her hair pulled back tight, with a black horsehair switch in a bun at her neck, her felt hat pushed back above her bangs, a Lalique circlet serving as a belt, her snob's skirt baring socks and high-button boots with cruel skate-runners, the actress, as violent as a curse in Hebrew, held herself straight and stiff at the edge of the rink, in the pose of someone undergoing an attack of nerves."[60]

---

[60] Jean Cocteau, *Portraits-Souvenir, op. cit.*

162. *Portrait of Polaire.* Photograph by Manuel.

---

[59] *Ibid.*

116

The Wasp Waist

The passage of Polaire, a meteor that was an omen, overturned the habits and the tastes of her time. She is the exact opposite of La Goulue, who reigned before her, a buxom popular sovereign whose perverted frenzy during the quadrille allowed one to glimpse, in the lightning flash of a raised leg, the fleeting vision of vaguely suspect paradises. In La Goulue's time, people like their women plump, with heavy bosoms and generous backsides. "Everything that makes the body thinner makes the skin looser," Dr. Caufeynon writes. "It is important, therefore, not to allow oneself to get thinner."[61]

Twenty years ahead of fashion, Polaire wears short hair and makes slimness triumph: her legendary waist fits in a man's size seventeen detachable collar. Above all she openly calls the attention of the new century to what the preceding century had persistently hidden: the attraction of slimness, the power of frail figures, the reign of extreme youth over aged, debauched, cynical ogres.

Aside from the glory he reaped from her, Claudine represented to Willy a business that had to be exploited as long as possible. For a decade there was hardly a revue at the end of the year, in cabarets, in music halls, in café concerts that did not have an act where "Willy" appeared, personified by some plump, seasoned actor, and a "Claudine," a role young "white hopes" fought for.

Other Schoolgirls

After the *Claudine* books came *Minne*, followed by *Les Égarements de Minne* [Minne's Misbehavior], the last products of the Willy-Colette association. Then came

---

[61] Dr. Caufeynon, *Le Conseiller secret des Dames* (Paris: H. Daragon, 1903). Caufeynon is the anagram of Fauconey, several of whose works are signed Jaf.

163. *Polaire.* Alastair. 1905.

Mady écolière [Mady the Schoolgirl], and later *Le Fruit vert* [Green Fruit], whose eroticism was less subtle. But tastes changed over a third of a century, and when Willy died in 1931 at the age of seventy-five, the fat, cynical Don Juan of the Gay Nineties was only a phantom and his books almost forgotten.

Claudine was, naturally, not the first heroine to incarnate the charms of adolescence. Among many other books, there was Catulle-Mendès' *Femme-Enfant* [The Childlike Woman] in 1891, and the considerable success, in 1894, of Marcel Prévost's *Demi-Vièrges* [Semi-Virgins] should not pass unmentioned, these *demi-vièrges* being vamps from good families whose lovers may enjoy them as they would shameless hetaerae, so long as they never force the last door.

But apparently it was after 1900 and Claudine that there appeared a mechanical sort of literature, spotlighting schoolgirls and

164. *Women.* Gustave Klimt. 1903.

their teachers, abused orphan girls, mothers who are streetwalkers, god-daughters who are too naïve, and the whole gamut of sensual terrors and joys that make puberty a troubled age.

Generations of schoolboys of all ages flushed with rather shamefaced happiness at the tale of the loves of Princess Aline and the dancer Mirabelle, in the country of Trypheme where King Pausole reigns.[62]

To catch their readers' eye novelists open the door of the dormitory a crack. "At nine o'clock one evening, while Laure and I were talking quietly in our beds, our hands intertwined, I dared, in the face of the bold gaze turned beseechingly on me, to let my fingers creep up her arm like a spider. Laure stifled a cry, then, half swooning, did the same to me. I too felt a shiver which went down to my private parts. And thus for many a long evening 'spiders' crept up our arms. Three weeks afterward they went as high as the shoulder, made their way across it, and approached the breast."[63]

In this boarding school we are the witnesses of the harmless intimacies of Pierrette and her cousin Eva, in which their teachers,

[62] Pierre Louÿs, *Les Aventures du roi Pausole,* illustrated by Lucien Métivert (Paris: Fasquelle, 1906). *The Adventures of King Pausole,* C. H. Lumley, translator (Paris: The Fortune Press, 1929).

[63] Antonin Reschal, *Pierrette en Pension* (Paris: Albin-Michel, 1904).

165. Drawings by Lucien Métiver for *Les Aventures du roi Pausole* by Pierre Louÿs. 1900.

119

166. "Maybe you would have liked my mother better!" Drawing by Forain.

von Kahlenberg's *Petite Sirène* [Little Siren], Pierre Corrard's *L'École des Maîtresses* [The School for Teachers], Adolphe Davant's *L'Initiatrice* [The Initiator], and the run-of-the-mill collections by Fort, Daragon, Juven, Méricant, Nillson, or Offenstadt.

The Little Monster

In the streets an increase in juvenile prostitution is the counterpart of these libidinous consumer products for which there is a greater and greater demand. With the power and animation of the most penetrating Constantin Guys drawings, Jean Lorrain in *Monstrillon* [The Little Monster] has traced for us the unforgettable portrait of a young strumpet: "... the fake schoolgirl with her fingers purposely stained with ink, with one chaste braid with a bright ribbon on it, Monstrillon, the horrible little prostitute who

Mademoiselle Levert, Miss May, and Miss Maud occasionally figure, with a more devouring passion. Less subtle than the *Claudine* books, the *Pierrette* books linger lovingly on caresses and embraces: "Every time that Evan met me during the day, her hand brushed against my cheek in a protective caress, and her words titillated my soul. Then she embraced me, and during the night that followed, I was invaded by a lingering voluptuousness, as if a rain of little kisses were falling on my flesh."[64] It must be admitted that Antonin Reschal, to whom we owe not only the *Pierrette* series but also the *Journal d'un amant* [Diary of a Lover], *Désirs pervers* [Perverted Desires], and a very useful *Guide des Plaisirs à Paris* [A Guide to Paris Pleasures], has a certain sly cleverness. We descend to a much lower level when we glance at contemporary works such as H.

[64] *Ibid.*

167. "Ah, Monsieur le Comte, how late you've kept our Nini out! She's going to miss her lesson at the Conservatory again." Drawing by Forain.

is taught the tricks of the trade by her mother, who carries the foul aura of lust with her all through the city and proceeds, a titillating aphrodisiac brushing lightly past, to solicit with her hips and elbows the groping senile hands that six years ago closed spasmodically around the bruised neck of little Neut."[65]

---

[65] This is a reference to a sadistic murder in 1900 which badly frightened "decent" families.

Lorrain meets Monstrillon in a first-class railway car on the Vincennes-Nogent-Joinville line, where he finds himself alone with her. "Twelve or thirteen years old at most, with a square of black serge over a little percale dress, her chest flat, a fifteen-*sou* straw hat on a young woman's stubborn, bulging forehead, and down her back the inevitable braid and its bit of ribbon, a lure that apparently salacious old men find irre-

168. *Offering.* A. Rouveyre.

169. "With a bosom like that aren't you ashamed
that your mother's still a concierge!" Drawing
by Frédéric Front. 1900.

sistible; with a briefcase under her arm...
the costume of a little girl going to school
or coming back from her lessons."

Monstrillon's gaze impudently seeks out
that of her traveling companion; she makes
faces, begins flirting with him. Then, chang-
ing tactics, she begins to play with the little
dog she has with her. "Monstrillon played
with this dog, hugged it in her arms, buried
it in her lap, devouring it with kisses, avid
caresses everywhere—on its muzzle, on its
ears, on its belly—as if overcome with an
insane need to love, and with each kiss her
gaze met mine, her eyes bored into me ob-
sessively, and her pale, pale mouth smiled.
There was better yet to come: as she frolicked
about, she had lolled back, stretching out
full-length on the seat, not caring that her
dress was pulled up, and her frail legs,
sheathed in black stockings, stuck out like
two shadowy pistils from the gaping calyx
of her petticoats; and as she played this mad

170. *The Fake Schoolgirl.* After *Die Erotik in
der Photographie,* Vienna, 1903.

game with her young animal, her knee kept grazing mine, her calves wound in and out between my legs, so as to call forth an apology, an 'oh, I beg your pardon' that would begin a conversation between us, in the desert of this stifling railroad car."[66]

Lorrain, who had a greater gift than anyone else for seeing and describing female sensuality, was not attracted by women of any age. Though he sought out their company—and had female friends that were faithful to him to the very end—he preferred side-show strongmen, tattooed workers from Billancourt, hotel porters, or stevedores for his amorous escapades. It is thus quite understandable that Monstrillon was nothing but an object to be observed, and in a sense an object of horror. But what man, provided he were not rooted to the spot by fear, could have resisted the vile temptation of a furtive escapade with this diabolical imp that he describes?

We are far from the radiant Polaire, magnified by the footlights, not even conscious, in her naïve euphoria, of the demons she awakens. We are entering the gloomy, shadowy zone where Monstrillons are fashioned. Factories, workshops, laundries, offices—sheer misery—fling pitiful fodder to venal love. The people toil and sweat and in the promiscuity of the slums their innocence soon fades. And then there are mothers, too many of them, for whom a female child is idle capital which they are anxious to have bear fruit.

Countless pages of such satiric newspapers as the *Assiette au beurre*, the *Gil Blas*, and *Rire* testify to the fact that this age was also that of satyrs. Popular songs also confirm this, as is evident from one of Mayol's successes, "La Polka des Trottins" [The Errand-Girl's Polka], with lyrics by Trebitsch and music by Christiné, first sung at La Scala in 1903:

[66] Jean Lorrain, *Une Femme par Jour* (Paris: Borel, 1906).

Gentils trottins ouvrez les yeux
Prenez bien garde aux vieux monsieurs.

[Nice little errand-girls, open your eyes
Be sure and watch out for old men.]

Little Girls

Though a somewhat superficial witness, Georges Brandimbourg has his facts right, and he has painted an impressive picture of juvenile prostitution at the end of the century. "A man who chases after little girls," he writes, "chooses them between nine and thirteen years old. If they are younger, their curiosity is not depraved enough, and if they are older, he often feels ashamed of himself."[67]

After this preamble, whose cold precision sends a shiver up the spine, Brandimbourg classifies the available girls:

[67] Georges Brandimbourg, *Croquis du Vice, op. cit.*

171. *Vice.* L. Vallet.

1. *The little beggar-girl,* dirty, disgusting, plying her trade on the outer boulevards, the environs of the Buttes-Chaumont, the fortifications, principally between the porte de Vitry and the porte de Gentilly, and the Vincennes quarries; and farther out, the porte de Moulineaux, Bicêtre, Gentilly, Vincennes, Quatre-Chemins, Saint-Ouen, and Clichy. In general they are directly exploited by their parents.

2. *The little flower-girl,* circulating in all quarters; the soil she grows best in is in places where there are many saloons for women (she is often debauched by these women). She is a little cleaner, without being particularly refined.

3. *The little nymph*; she chooses the elegant quarters. During the day she can be found on the main boulevards, on the Champs-Élysées, on the avenues leading to the Bois, near the Gare du Nord and the Gare de l'Est, on the square facing the Trocadéro, on the boulevard Henri-Martin, and in the Bois de Boulogne, and along the fortifications ditch. Her particu-

173. *"Darling, you have surpassed yourself,"* from *Pictures from the Boudoir of Madame CC,* portfolio with thirty drawings by Choisy le Conin (Franz von Bayros).

172. "I know Monsieur le Baron is not in the habit of buying a pig in a poke." Drawing by J. Wely. 1903.

lar trade marks: a short skirt, hair falling down her back and knotted near the nape of the neck by a bright-colored ribbon, a bow of the same color on her head, almost always wearing stockings, and ribbons of the same color. Her general appearance is clean; her walk is that of a respectable young woman; she walks faster on the main boulevards where she stops in front of shops only when she thinks she has a "trick to turn" following behind her. She goes home with him and into certain hotels, or "takes a ride" for two to three *louis*. Taking the hansom cab, she gets in and says aloud (for the coachman's benefit): "Get in first, Papa." She doesn't even bother to offer a bouquet of flowers. With one swift glance she sizes up how much the customer is worth, follows him or gets followed without exchanging a word. She is from thirteen to fifteen years old. "Industrialists" exploit these girls, unless they already belong to old bawds who have retired several times.

4. *The streetwalker,* in an outfit halfway between the *beggar-girl* and the *flower-girl,* works

only at night. So as not to attract the attention of the police, she has no particular trade-mark to distinguish her; for the same reason she often is accompanied by an elderly woman. She knows all the brothels, all the bawdy houses, and never mistakes an upright citizen for a policeman on the vice squad. In the daytime she parades her little sister about, which does not prevent her from waggling her haunches, if need be, to get money to buy pastry. She plunks her little sister down in a corner, and everything is all set.

We thought it best to quote this description at length; the style is a little heavy, but the facts are true, and it furnishes us with a poignant map of child prostitution in Paris.

A number of scandalous facts regarding debauchery of minors came out in court cases. Examples may be found in Paul Roué's book, *A huis clos, causes salées* [Spicy Cases Behind Closed Doors], published by Offenstadt in 1903. There is, moreover, hardly a periodical in which cartoonists do not treat this theme, from Forain to Steinlin, from Balluriau to Roubille. It seems to us that we are not exaggerating when we consider the taste for "green fruit," in the form in which we have just exhibited it, to be a characteristic phenomenon of the time.

It is a long way, certainly, from Claudine to Monstrillon, but these two mirages are alike, erotic phantoms in whose presence hypocritical, concupiscent mustaches quiver and are licked by frock-coated predators whose high starched collars turn their faces beet-red.

174. *Youth.* Auguste Renoir. Marquis de Bolli Collection, Paris.

175. *The Stairway*. Toulouse-Lautrec.

V.

GALLANT WOMEN

On the old melodies of Lulli,
We embark for Cythera,
Louveciennes or Marly.

Jean Lorrain

Streetwalkers, demimondaines, cocottes, tarts, whores, strumpets: the great army of Eros is on a war footing, a sidewalk infantry, a camouflaged artillery corps garrisoned in brothels, a plumed cavalry regiment along the boulevards, on the tree-lined avenues of the Bois, or on the Champs-Élysées.

The Army of Gallants

A draps ouverts [With Turned-Back Sheets]: this title of one of Willy's novels might have served as a motto for the regiments of courtesans, ranked in an unusually strict hierarchy that ranged from staff officers to foot soldiers. Unlike male armies, however, advancement in this army decreases in direct proportion to length of service.

After Daniel Defoe, Restif de la Bretonne, Balzac, and Eugéne Sue, naturalist novelists made the prostitute a heroine. Nana and Boule de Suif replace Camille and Mimi as popular favorites. Thanks to Maupassant and Lorrain, *La Maison Tellier* [Madame Tellier's Place] and *La Maison Philibert* [Madame Philibert's Place] opened their shutters and the inner workings of brothels came to light.

Around 1900, gallantry occupies an immense territory. It has its glorious female marshals, queens of the day whose favors are bought with a matched pair of horses or a diamond necklace. It also has its unknown soldiers, those humble and obscure figures who must be content with a five-franc piece or a few *louis* put down on the night-

176. *In Bloom.* Gustave Klimt. Drawing. 1904.
Albertina Graphische Samlung, Vienna.

177. *In Front of the Fireplace.* André Derain. Marquis de Bolli Collection, Paris.

178. *The Bath.* Stereoscopic photograph.

table next to the candle-holder. To their number are added occasional recruits, bourgeois women who are above reproach but give in when their "good friend" makes them a little present.

Greater and Lesser Cocottes

Balzac's Carabines and Esthers, instruments of the occult power of the Thirteen, have been replaced by beauties with a veneer that comes from frequenting princes. Liane de Pougy, whose real name was Anne-Marie Chasseigne, died Princess Ghyka. Émilienne d'Alençon, whose real name was Émilienne André, manages to get herself kidnapped by the Duke d'Uzès and seduced by the Duke d'Orléans, the Prince of Sagan, and King Leopold II, one after the other. Through its elegance and splendor, the gallant nobility eclipses genuine nobility, and likewise practices *noblesse oblige.*

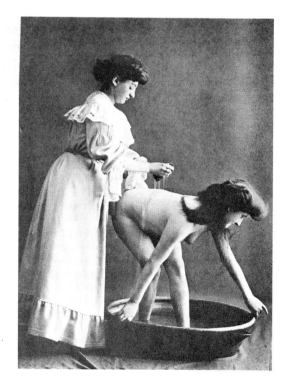

179. *The Tub and the Sponge.* Postcard.

180. *Jane Avril.* Edgar Chahine. Drypoint.
"And I have a heart as heavy
As the heart of a Damascene lady."
Guillaume Apollinaire

181. *Before the Bath.* Postcard. 1904.

182. *The Fine Shower.* After *Le Panorama, op. cit.*

Armon and Gerbidon's amusing comedy *L'École des Cocottes* [The School for Cocottes] depicts, some years later (1918), the spectacular rise of one of these demimondaines, who is taken in hand by a titled Pygmalion; in the last act, conscious of her duty, she sacrifices her personal happiness to her mission as an apostle. Armande Cassive, Jeanne Marnac, and Spinelli all lent their charm and their talent to this role.

This is also the world in which, twenty years earlier, on the tiny stage of the Théâtre des Nouveautés, Georges Feydeau tangled everything up in his hilariously complicated misunderstandings and impossible imbroglios, in *La Dame de Chez Maxim's* [*The Girl from Maxim's*] in 1899. Young Cassive was a

183. *The Ladies' Bath*. Le Quesnay.

184. *The Bidet*. Edgar Degas. Monotype.

tremendous success in it in the role of the Crevette brat, who appears again, married to some Eastern potentate or other, in *La Duchesse des Folies-Bergère* [The Duchess of the Folies-Bergère], staged in the same theater in 1902.

"Come on now, he's not my father!"— this shout, accompanied by a toss of the leg or a pirouette, was the rallying cry for the Léa des Glaieuls, the Renée la Jolies, the Eglantines, the Chouchous and the Lianes (these latter were legion) who tossed off champagne at Maxim's and somewhat tipsily danced on the tables to the rhythm of the famous chorus:

> Ta ma ra boum dié
> Ta ma ra boum dié
> Chahutez! Chahutez!
> Y a que ça pour bien s'porter!

> [Ta ma ra boum dié
> Ta ma ra boum dié
> Keep things in an uproar
> That's the only way to feel good!]

Care of the Body

These ladies perfumed themselves with opoponax and witch hazel, used L. T. Pivert, Azuréa, or Pink Clover Lotion, or else Pinaud's Precious Violet. They were the first to use such aids to cleanliness as the bidet —that is still unknown in Anglo-Saxon countries—and the Marval rotary-jet syringe was more frequently used in their residences than in the elegant Faubourg.

In a charming book, Countess Jean de Pange recounts her memories of her aristocratic childhood; she was born a Broglie and

132

185. *The Turkish Bath.* Le Quesnay. Engraving by Dérambez.

186. *The Towel.* Boldini.

counts Madame de Staël among her forebears. In the château that the Countess lived in, as in her family mansion on the rue de Miromesnil in Paris, there were no bathrooms. The pitcher and the basin, and in special cases the tub, were aristocratic society's rudimentary toilet aids.[68]

The demimonde, like the courtesans of old, is meticulous about personal hygiene.

[68] Comtesse de Pange, *Comment j'ai vu 1900* (Paris: Grasset, 1963).

The *biches* [does], as they were sometimes called, create the feminine type that men are suddenly mad about. The graceful figure of Liane de Pougy, whose slenderness and litheness live up to her first name (which means "liana"), approached that of the androgynous beauties celebrated by the poets. Cléo de Mérode, who was never a demimondaine, but whose pure face and beautifully proportioned body dominated the dreams of her time, and Lanthelme, who died a tragic early

187. *Nude Study*. Félicien Rops. The Louvre, Paris.

death, were also slim. During their reign, dance halls, promenades, beer halls, and the Bois will see imitation Lianes and ersatz Cléos proliferate, just as suburbs and provincial villages today secrete multitudes of fake Brigitte Bardots.

Beauties in the Bois

When we read Jean Lorrain's account of returning from a walk in the Bois, we can almost see them. "These ladies are coming from Les Acacias where you hear: 'What a hot spell, my dear!' 'Not a single rabbit in the thickets!' 'The asparagus season is over!' And here come Berthe d'Aigremont, and Blanche d'Amerbourg, and Rosa d'Amerpicon and so on, all maneuvering in their victorias with a matched pair of horses (is that all?) beneath the indulgent half-interested gaze of grand and powerful gentlemen

188. *The Riding Lesson.* E. Mouton. Postcard.

of distinction, in dress suitable for taking the waters or even swimming in the ocean, with large gray hats they have been sporting for a week now." (July 10, 1887.)

The sultans of this strolling harem are the Max Lebaudys, the Boni de Castellanes, the Bischoffsheims, the Alexandre Duvals, the Cahen d'Anvers, the La Mazelières, the Maxime Dreyfuses, observed by the pitilessly keen eyes of their artist companions, Caran d'Ache, Sem, Capiello, Boldini, La Gandara, Léandre. And when a queen passes, the murmurs cease and all eyes are turned toward her, "golden silences slashed by flights of Spanish flies," as Albert Samain sang in his litanies of Lust.

Caroline Otéro, a Spanish dancer and occasional demimondaine, yielded her favors only when it pleased her to do so. Virtuous Parisians were highly indignant at the suicide of little Chrétien, who was so chagrined when *la belle Otéro* refused his ten thousand francs in exchange for a night of love that he killed himself. Jean Lorrain, for his part, defended her: "...Insults and threats have been heaped on Mademoiselle Otéro: people say she should have accepted the ten thousand francs and their possessor. Why, may I ask? Because Mademoiselle Otéro's occupation is receiving quite large sums from this person and that. And what difference does that make? Even if it is true, Mademoiselle Otéro has the right to choose, which implies the right to refuse, and in my opinion these ten thousand francs that she plainly disdained speak highly of this woman whom today all Paris decries." (May 21, 1894.)

Otéro had an ample figure, Émilienne d'Alençon was rather plump, and Jane Avril was tall and thin, like Cléo and Liane. Women who wished to resemble the latter took Bouty's Thyroidine to slim down; others attempted to flesh out their bosoms by taking Oriental Pills and Royal Mamilaire. As for the men, in order to be prepared for any un-

189. *Miming of Courtesans.* Edgar Degas.

190. *La Maison Tellier.* Edgar Degas. Bibliothèque Nationale, Estampes, Paris.

191. *Dancers.* Edgar Degas. Marquis de Bolli
Collection (Galerie de Poche), Paris.

expected opportunities to take the offensive, they were never without the fashionable aids to virility—Ourania Pills, Golden Pearls, Henri IV Grains, Viriline—not to mention Herculex or Electro-Vigor magnetic belts, which were said to do wonders for a man.

Shops that Sell Surprises

Women who in 1830 were called *lionnes* [lionesses] and *panthères* [pantheresses] were known as *dégrafées* [unhooked ones] and *vrilles* [gimlets] in 1890. All of them might be referred to as *persilleuses* or streetwalkers,

women who *persillent*—that is, solicit customers.

Chased from the elegant quarters of the city around 1840, the lionesses took refuge in the Bréda quarter, around Notre-Dame-de-Lorette, acquiring at this time the name *lorettes.* The stretch of Paris from the place Blanche to Saint-Georges, from the rue Pigalle to the rue des Martyrs, was long the perimeter of love for sale. "The sidewalks of these streets are rinsed with water out of basins," Mérimée said, and Murger added: "It rains spermatazoa there!"

But the area abandoned by the lionesses did not remain empty long. Odd firms tacked up their name-plates there, for instance this

192. *At Nini's*. Toulouse-Lautrec.

one, to be found on the rue d'Argentueil around 1880:

SUZANNE
Lingerie   Trousseaux
Fittings

These were veiled brothels, whose owner tactfully slips a card into the vest pocket of a possible client:

LÉA OF THE WHITE HOUSE
PERSON OF INDEPENDENT MEANS
33 rue de Laval

Little notices in plain sight, drawn up in a language that the initiate can easily decipher, offer special refinements: English les-

193. *Modesty*. Anonymous. Circa 1890. Private collection, Bordeaux.

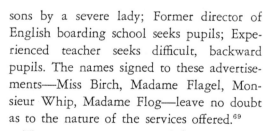

194. *Caroline Otéro.* Photograph by Reutlinger.

195. *Cléo de Mérode.* Postcard.

sons by a severe lady; Former director of English boarding school seeks pupils; Experienced teacher seeks difficult, backward pupils. The names signed to these advertisements—Miss Birch, Madame Flagel, Monsieur Whip, Madame Flog—leave no doubt as to the nature of the services offered.[69]

These apartments reserved for the secrets of furtive lovemaking, under fake signs advertising "Massages," "Lingerie," "Art Photographs," "Rare Books," "Japanese Prints," doubled as "marriage bureaus" and "booking agencies" which entrapped, usually with happy results, innumerable poor girls who had broken with their families and were weary of the workshop and its miseries.

"These houses," Georges Brandimbou writes, "of which there were one hundr fifty before 1870, saw an average of fi thousand girls pass through each yea Lorettes, Night-Beauties, Triflers, Cocotte and Strumpets. In 1890 this figure reache around twelve to fifteen thousand 'Horizo tal Ones,' 'Unhooked Ones,' 'Spraddle Ones,' 'Kneeling Ones,' 'Gimlets,' an 'Peapods.' Counting the seventy-five offici brothels of the capital (among them tw saloons enjoying the same prerogatives) r ceiving an average of nine hundred eigh women, the total comes to a respectab number."[70]

[69] Pierre Guénolé, *L'Étrange Passion* (Paris: H. Daragon, 1904).

[70] Georges Brandimbourg, *Croquis du Vic op. cit.*

The Street and Promenades

Outside of the establishments whose girls are subject to house discipline, there are the streetwalkers who size up the solvency of the "trick" at a glance, their prices varying from hour to hour. In the early evening they will settle for ten francs; during the hours of heaviest business they raise their prices to two or three *louis*. "I knew one," Charles Virmaître writes, "who never haggled. At her neck was a brooch with a portrait of good king Saint Louis in enamel. When the man asked her how much, she would show him her brooch. But I don't understand, he would say. My dear, she would reply, these

196. *Cléo de Mérode.* Photograph by Reutlinger.

197. *The Card Game.* Albert Guillaume.

198. *In the Bordello*. Félicien Rops.

199. *The Flea.* Matchbox cover. Luciano Emmer Collection, Rome.

are my arms that speak for me: *cinq louis*!"[71] *

No one has spoken more tenderly about the gallant "little friends" of the rue des Martyrs than Paul Léautaud, who spent his youth with them, sharing their secrets, listening to them tell how their days and their nights had gone, following them to the café or onto the promenades at night, in the bright lights of the music halls.

"Folies-Bergère, The Ice Palace, Casino de Paris, Olympia, Jardin de Paris, Marigny, and so many others, I walk through them in my mind's eye as if I were really there. The beauty of these bright, sparkling places, like brightly lighted squares. Once upon a time

[71] Charles Virmaître, *Paris-Impur* (Paris: Alfred Charles, 1900).

* In French, *cinq louis* [five *louis*] is pronounced exactly like Saint Louis. [Translator's note.]

200. *The Riding Crop.* Alastair. 1905.

201. *Woman with Cat.* Pierre Bonnard. Drawing. Private collection, Paris.

jewels, music, rowdy dances, libertinage, light-heartedness, leisure, heat, and rouge, for me are full of a charm and even an emotion that are like nothing else."[72]

Marcelle, Yvonne, Marthe, Lennie, La Perruche are "those who are weary before they start, those who cultivate desire without feeling it very much, and who go through nothing but the motions of love." These frivolous creatures, who never tired of "La Valse Bleue" [The Blue Waltz], "La Marche des Pierrots" [The March of the Clowns], or "L'Amant d'Amanda" [Amanda's Lover], smelled of patchouli, faded carnations, and Rachel Rose powder. They are the vagabond sisters of the inmates of bordellos dear to Degas and Lautrec.

[72] Paul Léautaud, *Le Petit Ami* (Paris: Mercure de France, 1902).

202. *The Big Number*. Xavier Sager.

there were Élysées-Montmartres, Ambassadeurs, Tivoli-Vauxhalls, Skatings, Boules Noires; and also Mabilles, Casinos, Courtilles, Closeries, Reines Blanches; a very long time ago Frascatis, Valentinos, Prados; and long, long ago Idalies, Tivolis, Folies, Paphos. All these names, which express and evoke a nervous, fast-paced life, a life of

203. "I see you've got the Legion of Honor. Did you expel some sisters?" H. Gerbault.

204. *Sparkling Wine.* Postcard.

it, syphilis is the real *"mal du siècle,"* for it corrupts the flesh and drives minds mad.

Prostitution and its dramas and miseries have been the object of a more than abundant literature, the tail end of naturalism, in which the smutty vies with the lugubrious. The period will react to the nauseating naturalistic "slice of life" by retreating to an imaginary, evanescent past, nothing of which remains perceptible except the refinement of its passions and the delicacy of its fragrances.

The Miseries of War

The battalions of love for sale, however, are watched over by a quartermaster's corps that recruits, imprisons, punishes, and keeps accounts at the same time: *alphonses, dos-verts,* and *macquereaux* are the procurers; *procureuses, allumeuses, maquerelles* are the bawds. At the top of the heap, the former *allumeuse* becomes assistant madam, and the dutiful *alphonse* administers an important "house" in the provinces, frequented by local notables. Bubu of Montparnasse, the pimp in a famous novel of that name, also becomes a hero, of the regrettable sort.

The army of Eros, especially where its sharpshooters are concerned, is eaten away by many cancers. This is the time of the Dream rubber, the Brou injection, the Midy sandalwood preparation, the miraculous Gré-bert lotion. As Armand Lanoux rightly put

205. *Intoxication.* German postcard.

146

206. *In Private*. 1890. *La Vie Parisienne.*

207. *The Bath. 1880. La Vie Parisienne.*

Aphrodite

The innumerable caricatures of Zola's *Nana* and the Goncourts' *La Fille Elisa* [Miss Elisa] will be countered by a Pierre Louÿs with the iridescent, dreamlike hedonism of his Chrysis. In the preface he wrote for his *Aphrodite,* which might be considered to be a sort of manifesto, he exclaims: "Will we ever see the days of Ephesus and Cyrenaica return? Alas! the modern world is succumbing to a tide of ugliness. Civilizations are retreating northward, are entering the fog, the cold, the mud. How dark it is! A people clad in black circulates in stinking streets. What is it thinking of? One no longer knows, but our twenty-five years shiver at being exiled in the midst of old men."[73]

The young companion of André Gide and Paul Valéry, who frequents the Goncourts' loft and Mallarmé's Tuesday salon, disdainfully shakes off the "turn of the century" mud dirtying his fine boots. Happy and nostalgic, he dives into the Mediterranean air of pre-Christianity, purified by the sea and the sun: ". . . May it be permitted those who forever regret not having known this intoxicated youth of the earth to call on the life of antiquity, may it be permitted them to relive, in fruitful illusion, the time when human nudity . . . could be unveiled beneath the features of a sacred courtesan . . . may it

be permitted them . . . to rebuild the Great Temple to the sound of magic flutes and enthusiastically dedicate, at the sanctuaries of the true faith, their hearts ever called onward by the immortal Aphrodite."

All the wanderings of Eros in *La Belle Epoque* shuttle between these two extreme shores: reality, cold, tattered (in a moral sense), held together by cynical and sordid loves, and the idealistic, unreal escape toward a dreamlike Middle East, toward a "somewhere else" where the Sphinx and the Chimera reign.

[73] Pierre Louÿs, *Aphrodite* (Paris: Mercure de France, 1896). English translation (New York: The Three Sirens Press, 1932).

208. *A pink and black jewel.* Alastair.

209. *The Woman with the Skeletons*. Gustave-Adolphe Mossa. Watercolor. 1906.

VI.

VICE AND MIRAGE

> I seek new perfumes, flowers opening
> wider, pleasures never before experienced.
>
> Flaubert

The long wavy hair, the frothy nudity, and the floral delirium that are the essence of Art Nouveau attempt to deny the hard realities of life. Many men and women of this time experience a burning need to lift anchor, a desperate, naïve desire to feel like naiads, fauns, fairies, or even flowers.

Flowers

"Roses! He absolutely had to have roses," Anatole Baju cries in 1886 in his periodical, *Le Décadent,* which is supported by Paul Verlaine. "Proud black irises, I am a fervent admirer of your shadows," Jean Lorrain, the poet of *Modernités,* murmurs, while the "leader of sweet odors," the celebrator of *Hortensias bleus* [Blue Hortensias], Robert de Montesquiou, announces:

> Les orchidées
> Sont décidées
> Aux plus étranges fantaisies.
>
> [Orchids
>   Have set their hearts
>   On the strangest fantasies.]

Here is how Jean Lorrain compares flowers to flesh after a visit to the Horticultural Salon, as it is about to close its doors: "This final agony is here aggravated by corruption. Withered and faded, but wilted in an equivocal sort of way, the mauve and yellow orchids [are] as crumpled as tissue-paper, the leaves of the caladiums fragile and transparent. The broad stars of the clematitis are still holding their own, like dull blue pupils of the eye, and the ripening roses insist on blooming: these bruised flowers emit a disturbing aroma. But in this first stage of decomposition, the rarest shades, the most curious gems are furnished by the irises. The browns and the dark blues, *Flamme-de-Punch* and *Duc-de-Flandre,* give off, alongside the putrescence of the yellows, the bluish splendors of a charnel house, those charnel houses in the manner of Gustave

210. *Gallant Women.* Cover for *Twenty Women* by Jean Lorrain.

Moreau, in which, on the liquefied heaps of cadavers, the genius of the painter evokes the gold-enameled slenderness of his diadem-crowned Helens." (May 25, 1895.)

Brain Fever

The disturbing beauty of dying flowers, the traumatizing horror of battlefields and scenes of torture into which Octave Mirbeau leads his terrified strollers in the *Jardin des Supplices* [The Torture Garden], the incestuous loves of Giulia and Ulric d'Este, recounted by Elémir Bourges in his *Crépuscule des Dieux* [The Twilight of the Gods], the monstrous couplings in the time of Ellagabal, minutely incised in *Agonie* [Agony] of Jean Lombard, the bitter joys of Lesbos and Sodom, orgies and rapes, improbably tortured

and torturing loves; such are a few of the ingredients that make up the erotic elixir of "turn of the century" intellectuality.

Without a trace of humor, with a conviction that would be offended by the slightest smile, Xavier Privas raises his voice in song:

Les Chimères sont des Oiseaux
Qui volent autour des Cervelles,
Les Chimères sont des Oiselles
Qui volent autour des Cerveaux.

[Chimeras are male birds
That circle brains,
Chimeras are female birds
That circle minds.]

Echoing the weighty agonies of Huysmans' decadent hero Des Esseintes as if he were answering him, Rémy de Gourmont writes *Sixtine,* subtitling it "a novel of cere-

211. "Wolff's Choice," the cigar of high society.

212. *The Siren.* Armand Point. 1897. *La Plume.*
"I dreamed of you in the naïveté of things"
Henry Bataille

213. *Harpy carrying off a dead poet.* Gustave-Adolphe Mossa. Watercolor. 1907. Musée Jules Chéret, Nice.

"O woman, a kiss would slay me
If beauty were death..."

Mallarmé

bral life." Contorted, sensitive, possessed of a light touch, this book is nielloed with tender and disabused little poems:

Il pleuvait des plumes de paon
Pan, pan, pan,
La porte multicolore s'embrasa de flammes,
Le ciel de lit trembla vers un oarystis,
Il pleuvait des plumes de paon
De paon blanc.[74]

[It rained peacock feathers
Plink, plink, plink,
The multicolored door burst into flame,
The bed-canopy trembled toward an oarystis,
It rained peacock feathers
From a white peacock.]

---

[74] Rémy de Gourmont, *Sixtine* (Paris: Mercure de France). *Very Woman,* English translation by J. L. Barrets (New York: N. L. Brown, 1922).

And the hero, d'Entragues, mourns not knowing "that Rome of the Popes, that womb of the Ideal, that Babylon of the Cross, that Sodom of mysticism, that arch of sadistic dreams, that incunabulum of sacred madnesses, that generatrix of a new kind of passion. . . ."

At the Ambassadeurs, Yvette Guilbert in her scalpel-like-voice cuts through the refrain of the song "La Decadante" [The Decadent Woman]:

Symboliste,
O, puriste!
Femme au regard troublant
La paleur de tes joues
Me prouve que tu joues
De la flûte, de la flûte, de la flûte de Pan!

[Symbolist,
O purist!
Woman with the disturbing gaze
The paleness of your cheeks
Proves that you play
The flute, the flute, the flute of Pan!]

214. *The Siren's Song.* Franz von Bayros. One of ten illustrations to *The Fairy Tale of All Fairy Tales* or *The Pentameron* by Giambattista Basile.

154

215. *The Effrontery of Prostitutes*. Alastair.
1905.

"Modernity, Modernity
Amid cries and hoots
The effrontery of prostitutes
Gleams in eternity."

Jean Lorrain

217. *Gay Paree.* Postcard. 1901.

Here, as always, there is a double meaning: in its subtleties as in its vulgarities, *La Belle Epoque,* the era of Art Nouveau, plays on words, with words, around words, games of hide-and-seek between exhibitionists and voyeurs who get a choicer pleasure by multiplying the veils.

The Spread of Vice

Vice, with a capital V, the shame and terror of the solid citizen, exerted a powerful attraction. Today the word has become watered down, but in this era it was still a very strong word. Bookstores displayed volumes with tempting titles: Joséphin Péladan's *Le Vice Suprême* [The Supreme Vice]; Jean Lorrain's *Le Vice Errant* [Errant Vice]; Georges Brandimbourg's *Croquis du Vice* [A Quick Sketch of Vice]; Victor Joze's

216. Illustration by Clara Tice for *Aphrodite* by Pierre Louÿs.

218. Postcard. Circa 1900.

Paris-Gomorrhe [Paris-Gomorrah]; Henri d'Argis' *Sodome* [Sodom]; Victorien du Saussay's *L'École du Vice* [The School for Vice]; Jules Davray's *L'Armée du Vice* [The Army of Vice]; Dr. Fauconey's *Les Vices féminins* [Vice in Women]; J. de Merlin's *Vice, crime, amour* [Vice, Crime, Love]; Louis Besse's *La Débauche* [Debauchery]; Saint-Médard's *La Volupté féroce* [Ravenous Sensual Pleasure]; Serge Paul's *Le Vice et L'Amour* [Vice and Love]—and this is only a small sample.

In 1884, *Monsieur Vénus* appears in Brussels, published by Brancart and signed by both Rachilde and Francis Talman. "This bizarre book will be read and will make us think," the anonymous critic of the *Tintamarre* writes. "It is a dreadful, disturbing symptom of this green-tinged decomposition we are foundering in." And Colombine, in the *Gil Blas,* is indignant: "Do you know

219. *Portrait of Rachilde.* Circa 1886.

220. *Judith* from *La Bonbonnière,* an "Amorous
and Curious Collection of Erotic Fantasies" by
Choisy le Conin (Franz von Bayros), with "Para-
phrases in Poetry and Prose" by Amadee de la
Houlette.

221. *Garters.* Retouched photograph. Robert Giraud Collection, Paris.

Maurice Barrès. "What is most subtle about the perversion of this book," Barrès writes, "is the fact that it was written by a twenty-year-old girl."

A scandalous Amazon, Rachilde seems to want to make each of her novels more shocking than the last. In *La Marquise de Sade* [The Marquise de Sade] (1887), *Madame Adonis* (1888), *Monsieur Vénus* (1889), *L'Animale* [The Female Animal] (1893), *L'Heure sexuelle* [The Hour of Sex] (1898), *Les Hors Nature* [Those Beyond Nature] (1903), her heroes and heroines raise the sick sensibilities and the nervous irritation of "decadent" estheticism to the point of paroxysm.

Born Marguerite Eymeri, Rachilde became Madame Alfred Valette and with her hus-

what her book, her story is about? A new commentary on Sappho's verses? Come, come, she herself tells us that Sappho is old hat and that Lesbos can be found on any street corner. This is the story of a woman who marries and through a frightful, all-encompassing perversion turns her husband into a woman and herself into a man. This is what a twenty-year-old girl invents, what she dreams of!"

Rachilde

In 1889, the same book is republished by Genonceaux, signed this time by Rachilde alone and accompanied by a preface by

222. *A Leaf of the Female Vine.* (Before Marcel Duchamps.) 1892.

band reigned over the *Mercure de France.* Jean Lorrain, who was very fond of her, drew this portrait of her in 1884: ". . . a schoolgirl with a sober and reserved manner, very pale to be sure, but it is the pallor of a studious schoolgirl, a genuine young girl, a bit thin, a bit frail, with the grave profile of a Greek ephebus or a young Frenchman in love . . . and eyes—oh, her eyes! they are huge, with unbelievably thick lashes and clear as water, eyes that know nothing, that lead you to believe that Rachilde does not see with these eyes, but rather has others in the back of her head to seek out and discover the fiery spices with which she seasons her works."[75]

It is quite true that the super-erotic imagination of this extraordinary creature knows no bounds. *Les Hors Nature,* for example, is about a case of incest, a subject that even in this era was considered quite scabrous. But the reader must beware; he must not think that he is about to witness love scenes between brother and sister. Not at all; it is about two *brothers* tied to each other by a monstrous passion, one of whom will kill the other and then commit suicide in a house that they have purposely set on fire. Here is a passage from the book: "Paul-Eric de Fertzen was getting dressed. Silver reflectors focused on his handsome face the blinding

[75] Jean Lorrain, "Mademoiselle Salamandre," *Le Courrier Français*, November 1, 1884. This article marked Lorrain's début as a journalist.

rays of stark-white electric corollas, a bouquet of glorious lilies whose cruelly cold light glorified him in a pure apotheosis. Slim and lithe, the very young man contemplated himself in profile, with a feline torsion of his trunk that made his hip curve out, and with slow gestures, stretching his arm out deliberately, he went to meet his double. His head

223. *The Supreme Vice.* Alastair. 1905.
"Oh! Astral intoxication!"

Péladan

160

224. *Salome.* Aubrey Beardsley. 1896.

thrown back, his eyes half closed and quivering with a voluptuous blinking of his eyelids, drinking himself in, intoxicated with
himself, he raised his face, pallid with pride,
and tilted it backward, and the two black
stains formed by the shadow of his nostrils,
little palms of funereal velvet, alighted on
the dazzling whiteness of his complexion, like
a macabre reminder to scorn the body. 'Eric,'
Jacques Reuther de Fertzen said in a grave,
somewhat muffled voice, 'it is ridiculous to
preen like that.' "[76]

The Middle East

Narcissism, nymphomania, Sapphism, opi-
um, ether, absinthe: the Eros of *La Belle
Epoque* is shot through with visions and
mirages. The cruel refinements of the em-

[76] Rachilde, *Les Hors Nature* (Paris: Mercure
de France, 1903).

161

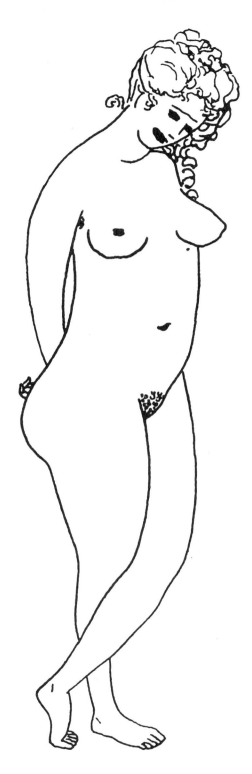

225. *Ohh!* A. Rouveyre.

226. *"Spermatorrheas of thoughts!"* Gustave Klimt. Private collection, Vienna.

perors of China, the lustful excesses of
Assyria and Babylon, the lubricious Pharaohs,
the wallowing in vice of the Eastern em-
perors, the wild orgies of the last Caesars:
this whole chaotic tissue of themes—more or
less supported by discoveries made through
a historical method that was still in its in-
fancy—fills the mustached and bearded heads
of daydreamers in the year 1900.

"The Middle East! The Middle East!"
Rachilde cries. "A queen with little bare feet.
You, the all-powerful, the eternally prosti-
tuted! Adorable Cleopatra, whose private
parts, once you were dead, were gilded so as
to make them nothing more than an em-
blem of lucre and horror. . . . Exquisite princess, lithe maiden, serpent who wrapped
herself around Marc-Antony, the hard-
bitten old soldier, and made him fall . . .
naïve criminal, spouse of your brother or of

227. *Salome*. Aubrey Beardsley.

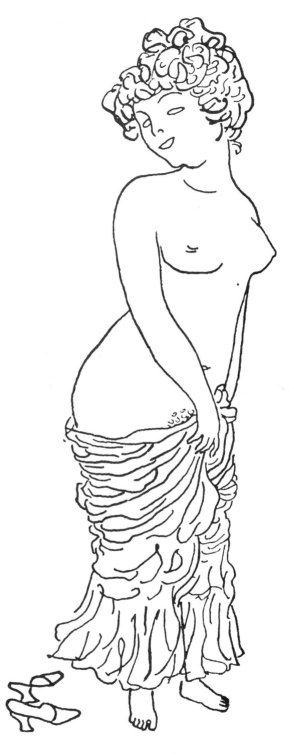

228. *Woman of the World*. A. Rouveyre.

163

229. *Evoe!* A. Rouveyre.

230. *The Middle East.* Postcard. Robert Giraud Collection, Paris.

your son, no one now quite knows which . . . but so virile that all the galleys fled to the open ocean of the pupils of your eyes . . . bouquet of brown and white roses with petals of iron, I salute you."[77]

Péladan the Seer, with his Assyrian beard and his magician's robe, surveys the tottering

West with his messianic gaze and denounces its mental lawlessness: "Oh," he cries, "the filthy onanism of thought . . . astral intoxication, the instinct of lust spurred on by the spirit of lust, the soul titillating the body! The habitual drunkenness of the senses is hideous; organic excess is shameful; but this! this! this is the *supreme vice.*"

The Supreme Vice

In the same novel, *Le Vice Suprême*, the hero, Mérodak, whom Péladan modeled after himself, is a grand Initiate with an inflexible will, a champion of monarchy and the catholicity of the medieval church. He stigmatizes

[77] Rachilde, *L'Heure sexuelle* (Paris: Mercure de France, 1898).

164

231. Christophe Henri Karel de Nerée tot Baberich. Sepia. 1900. Hessiches Landesmuseum, Darmstadt.

that she grows pale all over, she reins in her flesh."[78]

Mérodak, whose seer's eye penetrates the most secret thoughts and divines the most deeply buried desires, lectures his proud, unsatisfied beloved: "Guard against these pollutions by the imaginary," he tells her. "They lead to a spermatorrhea of thoughts.... The specters of your eroticism, Your Highness, will be the demonic incubuses of your obsession."

Such strange words. . . . We remember that Maurice Dekobra's novels of the twenties still bore the trace of this poisonous vocabulary and this broken syntax.

---

[78] Joséphin Péladan, *Le Vice Suprême* (Paris: 1884).

232. *The Necklace*. A. Rouveyre.

those whom he calls "knights of the depraved world." A princess desires him, but scorning the flesh, he resists. The love-smitten princess is reduced to solitary dreams: "In her titillating reverie, the princess feels overwhelmed by her dream and is submerged in it; beads of perspiration break out on her forehead, her ears grow red, and her earlobes tremble.... She has a nightmare: everything becomes obscene. Goats, cross-eyed with lust, break their horns in frantic caresses: an enfevered phallephoric procession passes; and the inner friezes of a temple of Priapus unfold, the Panathenaeae of the ignoble. . , . Suddenly, there is a break in the procession. Clinging to her pride with such an effort

Though Péladan had fervent admirers and even disciples, he nonetheless was a ridiculous figure in the eyes of some of his famous contemporaries. In his novel *Maîtresses d'Esthètes* [Mistresses of Esthetes], Willy's Sautaucrack is a caricature of Péladan (Rodolphe Salis had nicknamed Péladan "Ataxerfesse"). As for Jean Lorrain, he rejoices in one of his Pall-Mall columns because he has been too ill to attend the Seer's wedding, and therefore did not swell the ranks of the "parade of gynandrous lady painters, Princess Paules, ethopoetic magi, old lady spiritualists, esthete necromancers, and other bit-players from Paris's rotten high society." (January 11, 1896.)

Sphinx?

Brains are heated white-hot, minds are out of kilter, the sexes can't be told apart, instincts are deceiving, and desires gasp for breath. At the Jardin de Paris, Mademoiselle Misotten in 1906 introduces "Sphinx?" a waltz sung by Pierre Chapelle and Francis

233. "The woman with the jewels, the one who drives you mad..." Robert Giraud Collection, Paris.

234. *Women.* After *Die Erotik in der Photographie,* Vienna, s.d.

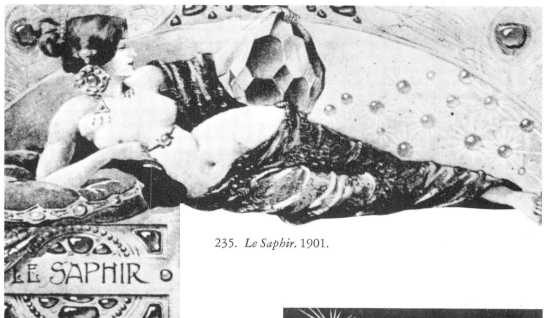

235. *Le Saphir.* 1901.

Popy, whose chorus betrays the nail-biting that went along with apprehensive Art Nouveau:

D'où viens-tu? Que veux-tu?
O créature étrange!
Tu parais un démon et pourtant tes youx sont
d'un ange.
Et malgré la douceur de ta voix de mésange,
Eloigne-toi, j'ai peur,
O sphinx enchanteur.

[Where do you come from? What do you
want?
O strange creature!
You look like a demon and yet your eyes are
angel's eyes
And despite the softness of your tomtit voice,
Go away; I'm afraid
O enchanting sphinx.]

The Sphinx and the Chimera, the hybrid, the androgyne, the vampire, the harpy: these fabulous beings people the mental orgies of esthetes intoxicated by the pre-Raphaelite

236. *Virgo.* (A constellation.) Postcard.

237. *Two Women*. Louise Hervieu. Drawing. Stephen Higgons Collection, Paris.

de Vespera" [The Princess of Vespera], "Artémise" [Artemis], "Viviane," "Rose d'enfer" [Rose from the Inferno], "Virginital," "Mélusine," "Désespoir de la Chimère" [The Chimera's Despair], "Primitive Diablesse" [The Primitive She-Devil], "Sort des Rêves" [The Lot of Dreams]! People blowing their lids, as Jarry would put it. And these people hum Saint Saëns or, failing that, the melodies of Ernest Chausson.

Qu'es-tu donc? Je ne sais, un ange, un démon,
une femme?
Que m'importe après tout, fais fleurir dans
mon âme
La joie ou le malheur
O sphinx enchanteur.

238. A pretext: *The kiss under the mistletoe*.
La Grande Vie, op. cit.

movement and Rosicrucian symbolism. It rains Ophelias; it snows Herodiases. Jean Lorrain, a tireless rhapsodist, sings of the uncertain loves of his *Princesses d'Ivoire et d'Ivresse* [Princesses of Ivory and Intoxication], of his *Princes de Nacre et de Caresse* [Princes of Mother-of-Pearl and Caresses]. Paintings by Armand Point, Alexandre Séon, Edmé Couty and some twenty others are hung in the 1895 Rosicrucian Salon. "In the presence of the Grail, the Seemly, and the Rose that Bears a Cross," the catalogue states. And the titles of the works: "Princesse

[What are you then? I don't know: an angel,
a demon, a woman?
But what does it matter to me after all;
Make joy or suffering
Burst into bloom in my soul
O enchanting sphinx.]

This is the end of the song whose first chorus we have quoted above. Joy or suffering; it makes no difference. The essential thing is to be fascinated. People passively surrender to obscure forces. To describe his irresistible hero, Péladan invented the word *méduseur,* "a turner to stone."

Dances of Ideas

Belle Epoque nervousness, doubtless aggravated by overgenerous doses of absinthe and

239. Illustration by Franz von Bayros for *Stories from Aretino.*

240. *Tango.* Raphaël Kirchner.

ether, brings on a curious sexual vagueness, a bewilderment of the senses, a confusion of the carnal and the psychic, in the face of which interdictions topple and the improbable becomes the norm. What we find in Christiné's song, "T'en souviens-tu Bichette" [Do you remember, Bichette?], introduced around 1905 by the irreplaceable Dranem, is doubtless an echo of such divagations:

Nous faisions de l'auto dans des champs de
    lotus
J'y laissai mon nombril, tu laissas ton ombrelle,
J'perdis mon numéro et toi ton humérus.
J'étais ton caillou rose et toi t'étais ma caille,
Et mordant sans pitié tes cheveux jusqu'au sang
Je me brisai trois dents à ton peigne
    d'écaille . . .

241. *Water games, a panorama of 1900.*

[We were driving through fields of lotuses
I left my navel there, you left your umbrella,
I lost my number there, and you lost your
    humerus.
I was your pink pebble and you were my quail,
And pitilessly biting your hair till it bled
I broke three teeth on your tortoise-shell
    comb . . .]

This is incoherent and unrestrained, certainly, but one wonders whether this parody sounds any more improbable than, say, a passage from *Un Inceste* [An Incestuous Affair], a novel by Valentine de Saint-Point, published at the author's expense around 1904, in which we find the following dialogue between an adolescent and his mother:

"You palpitate splendidly, every sort of harmony is within you, harmony itself is within you . . . Mother, Mother!"

"Siegfried . . ."

"Give me, O give me your breath so that our two bodies may breathe as one; far removed from others, may nothing ever separate us again, and may my youth become exacerbated in your unique flesh and my life exhaust itself. . . ."

Valentine de Saint-Point, whose real name was Valentine de Glaus de Cessiat-Vercell,[79] brought the "Dances of Ideas" to the stage in 1914; in them she gave a choreographic interpretation of her own poems, recited by a narrator, her face masked, her body clad in gold lamé.

Tu as enfermeé, nus, mes deux pieds dans ta
    main
Sur eux tu as posé ta tête . . . (etc.) [80]

[You enclosed my two bare feet in your hand
    You placed your head on them . . .]

Green Eyes

Ideas, chimeras, dreams, words: like sorceresses' brooms they bear minds off to Witches' Sabbaths where the senses exhaust themselves, where flowers are sex organs and mouths, where gems are eyes:

O les pierres, ces sans-paupières
Qui vous regardent fixement.
O les cent paupières, les pierres
Qui s'ouvrent démesurément.[81]

[O precious stones, those [eyes] without eyelids
    That stare at you.
    O the hundred eyelids, the stones
    That open inordinately.]

Monsieur de Phocas, Jean Lorrain's decadent hero who resembles the Des Esseintes of Huysmans, pursues the disappointing mirage of green eyes, the color of absinthe or

242. *A Woman Damned.* Pierre Bonnard.

[79] In 1913 she participates in the Futurist movement, writing the *Manifeste Futuriste de la luxure* [Futurist Manifesto on Lust].

[80] *Fantasio,* No. 179, January 1, 1914.

[81] Robert de Montesquiou, *Les Paons,* cover illustrated by Lalique (Paris: Fasquelle, 1901).

243. The Countess d'Urville at her masked ball on the avenue de l'Alma. After *La Grande Vie, op. cit.*

of the cold sea, throughout the world. "With the light of a gem before me, I am smitten, worse, spellbound, possessed by a certain sea-green transparency; it is like a hunger within me. I search in vain for this light in pupils and in precious stones, but no human eye possesses it."[82]

It is this very look that Lorrain came across in the eyes of a pale adolescent boy with a slender neck, whose ambiguous beauty he describes thus:

La tête douloureuse, ardente et maladive,
A, dans le morne attrait de sa grâce native,
Le charme d'une vierge et d'un garçon pervers.

Favori de prélat ou savante Ophélie,
Son énigme est souffrance, entraînement, folie
Et comme un philtre noir coule dans ses yeux
    verts.[83]

[His aching, burning, sickly head,
  In its gloomily attractive native grace
  Has the charm of a virgin and a depraved boy.

A prelate's favorite or a knowing Ophelia,
His mystery is suffering, witchery, madness
And something like a black philter flows in
    his green eyes.]

The ambiguity of the sexes, of desire, the reversal of poles, the transfer of feelings, the double meaning of gestures: all anomalies fuse in this palace of mirages of the exacerbated senses.

The haughty Renée Vivien, a woman poet, sings defiantly of Sapphic love:

Nos lunaires baisers ont de pâles douceurs,
Nos doigts ne froissent point le duvet d'une
    joue,
Et nous pouvons, quand la ceinture se dénoue,
Etre tout à la fois des amants et des soeurs.[84]

[82] Jean Lorrain, *Monsieur de Phocas* (Paris: Ollendorff, 1901).

[83] Jean Lorrain, *L'Ombre ardent* (Paris: Ollendorff, 1897).

[84] Renée Vivien, *A l'heure des mains jointes* (Paris: Sansot).

244. Two illustrations for *Amants Féminins,* a novel by Adrienne Saint-Agen, (Charles Offenstadt, Paris, 1904).

[Our moonlit kisses have pale sweetnesses,
  Our fingers do not bruise a downy cheek,
  And when our girdle is unknotted, we can
  Be at once both lovers and sisters.]

In love with love, Renée Vivien is a frail, apprehensive, unreal woman. Her apartment is lighted by candles and the light of day must filter through the thick panes of glass that isolate it from the noise of the street. Food repels her, she is diaphanous, she sings for her sisters: "You will be a stranger to the race of men ... Psappha will offer you the flower of her graces. Eranna will speak to you of Agatharchis and Myro, Nossis will plait her mauve irises for you.... You will be a captive of dreams and harmonies that have disappeared.... You will contemplate the white peplums of virgins who bend to

gather seashells as delicately mysterious as half-opened sexual parts."[85]

She lives in a casket that is padded to keep out noise and light, where the nudity of her friends is illuminated by the dull reflections of precious stones: "Madonna Gemma, you are well-named. You are the dazzling sister of precious gems.... I love seaweed that is the same soft color as your eyes.... How you sparkle in the shadows. Turn your beryl eyes from me...."

Jean Lorrain

Jean Lorrain would probably have liked the name Madonna Gemma, judging by the

---

[85] Renée Vivien, *La Dame à la Louvre* (Paris: Sansot).

173

245. "They made love so well that one evening A. found herself on the sidewalk." After *La Grande Vie, op. cit.*

sapphires and opals in his tie-pins, and the heavy rings, cameos and moonstones, that adorned his fingers. A tender Hercules with eyes the color of pale water, powdered and rouged beneath his disconcerting mustache, swaggering, biting, languishing, dreaming, he was tireless, and in his own way the incarnation of Nietzsche's maxim: "I am everything and I wish to be everything: serpent, dove, and pig."

Jean Lorrain, who has been cited more than any other author in the course of this book, not only had a photographic eye like Maupassant's; he also had the most subtle antennae and the privileged gift of feeling, understanding, and seeing in a double register: "Who, then," Paul Morand writes, "is as much a woman as this man when he speaks of women? He envies them their lovers, their way of dressing, their success in music halls; he goes straight to what flatters them or what is most apt to wound them; he buys toilet preparations at the same perfumer's; he has the same tastes: public executions, lace, the smell of wild beasts on the jacket of the animal tamer. Like them, he can bite and scratch, remain a child.... He is a woman in the way he gets drunk on ether, in his passion for knickknacks, in his great love of disguises and pseudonyms, in his vocation as an actor *manqué* ('I would adore to be a terrifying clown'), in his awkward, slanting writing. There is nothing masculine about him except the writer in him."[86]

[86] Jean Lorrain, *Femmes de 1900,* Préface de Paul Morand (Paris: Editions de la Madeleine, 1932).

246. Out-of-the-ordinary drawings from an "English" novel. Esbey.

This last sentence is unjust. Lorrain also has a man's courage: the courage to tell the truth, to proceed farther, regardless of what it may cost him; the courage to assume, like a *grand seigneur*, the role he has cast himself in, a role whose ridiculousness and disgracefulness escape him not at all; and courage, finally, in the face of suffering, which he endured without a murmur of complaint all during the cruel illness that killed him.

Lorrain was not only the dazzling chronicler of the spectacle of Parisian high society, but also the troubled researcher in dangerous parts of the city, dark alleyways, pale suburbs, vacant lots around the fortifications, regions beyond the pale where suffering and corrupted human beings toiled, human beings whom his searching eye sounds and scrutinizes with the precision of an impassioned botanist.

J'ai passé cette nuit entre deux débardeurs
Qui m'ont débarrassé de toutes mes ardeurs.

[I have spent this night between two stevedores
Who relieved me of all my burning desires.]

He cynically flings out these verses that are all the more provocative because they are the truth. Attacked one day, slashed with a knife, and stripped by three hoodlums in a disreputable hotel on the rue Galande, he wakes up naked underneath a filthy sheet. He sends word through a messenger to Rachilde at the *Mercure de France*. She rushes to him, gets him out of his predicament, and says nothing. Twenty years passed before she told of the incident.[87]

Jean Lorrain and the "Impénitent" that Verlaine sings of have a great deal in common:

Rodeur vanné, ton oeil fané
Tout plein d'un désir satané . . .[88]

[Weary prowler, with your faded eye
Full of satanic desire . . .]

An Aeolian harp whose strings tremble in the slightest breeze, Jean Lorrain, all by himself, gives us a concrete picture of the curiosities, the appetites, the wanderings, the exquisiteness, and the open wounds that are the very warp and woof of his time. If he makes things up, it is always to give us a glimpse of a land of enchantment: "He who has not believed when he is a child will never dream as a young man; on the very threshold of life we must dream of weaving beautiful dream-tapestries to decorate our

247. *Portrait of Jean Lorrain. La Grande Vie, op. cit.*

---

[87] Rachilde, *Portraits d'Hommes* (Paris: Mercure de France, 1921).

[88] Paul Verlaine, *Parallèlement* (Paris: Vanier, 1889).

248. Label for an American cigar. 1901.

dello, in *La Maison Philibert*; or yet again provides us with dozens of portraits from life, impeccably elegant, true snapshots, in *La Bockeuse* [The Girl in the Beerhall], *Monstrillon* [Little Monster], *Celle qui se tuera* [The Girl Who Will Kill Herself], *La Foraine* [The Girl from the Street Fair], imperishable sketches that make him the Constantin Guys of writing.

As a writer, Jean Lorrain belongs not behind, but at the side of those who were his masters, Huysmans and Barbey d'Aurevilly, both of them great lovers of monsters. When they first became friends, Barbey gave him a little brochure that evoked the incestuous loves of the Ravalets, in which he wrote this dedication: "To Jean Lorrain, what is not a monstrosity to him." Lorrain read it, and

lodging when winter approaches: and even faded dreams make sumptuous tapestries for December."[89] It is the author of *La Forêt bleue* [The Blue Forest], of *Narkiss*, of *Brocéliande*, and of *Yanthis* speaking: poems and stories that he has dreamed, that resemble the allegories of Gustave Moreau (whom he worships) and the jewelry of his friend René Lalique.

Elsewhere he commingles the imaginary and real life, getting down a magnificent portrait of Barbey d'Aurevilly, whom he calls Monsieur de Bougrelon, few of the details of which are imaginary; or else he leads us, in *Histoires de Masques* [Stories of Masks], into a world of visions and phantoms brought on by ether, which he absorbs so much of that he dies of it; or again he gives us precise reporting, with a realism that knows no excesses and is not pulled out of shape by complacency, of what goes on inside a bor-

[89] Jean Lorrain, *Princesses d'Ivoire et d'Ivresse* (Paris: Ollendorff, 1902).

249. *Ophelia*. Postcard.

250. "My costume is flimsy, so I wore a mask so that nobody would recognize me." H. Gerbault.

at Lachenal's shop: the ceramist whose misleading pottery glazed a gray-green the color of stagnant water is so unusually soft to the touch, as soft as the skin of a woman, but a woman who has been touched lightly in her most private parts."[91]

This is only a precious little note, a short halt before being overtaken by the night, a night from which he will often bring back the groans of a man wounded, the rattle of a man on his deathbed. Without being completely conscious of it, perhaps, for he was less a man of intellect than a man of instinct, he felt and lived the intimate fusion of horror and ecstasy that is the very fabric of eroticism: "from the most unavowable to the most lofty," said Georges Bataille, who recognized Jean Lorrain as one of the lords and masters in this area.

[91] July 4, 1897.

said to him, blushing: "Oh, maestro, you flatter me, but I have no sister!" and takes the volume home, he confesses, "absolutely delighted."[90]

He carefully keeps this unusual homage and later, commenting on his somewhat juvenile response, came up with this reflection, which has a fair measure of truth in it: "One is always proud of the vices one is said to have, though one is generally less proud of the ones one really has."

We have not strayed from our subject by devoting so much space to Jean Lorrain. We might almost say that he *is La Belle Epoque*, Art Nouveau, without thereby falling into paradox. His work is saturated with eroticism—the examples we have given are witness to this—no matter what subject he treats: the streets, flowers, clothes, a certain look, objects. Here he is talking of the ceramics of his friend Lachenal: "At Châtillon,

[90] Georges Normandy: *Jean Lorrain intime* (Paris: Albin-Michel, 1928).

251. *Variation on the Circus.* Toulouse-Lautrec.

252. *The Morphine Addict.* Eugène Grasset.
1900. N. V. Citroën Collection, Amsterdam.
"How many ambushes are concealed in this
trap that is turning blue!"
Georges Rodenbach

253. *Salome.* Pablo Picasso. J. M. Lo Duca Collection, Paris.

VII.

CURTAIN

I secretly gather mysterious flowers.
Paul Verlaine[92]

This oscillation from the ignoble to the sublime which is the fate of Eros was perhaps never so obvious as it was in these thirty years from 1880 to 1910 that have concerned us here, an era that was at once pedestrian and mad to reach the heights, cynical and innocent, greedy for gain and ruinously eating up its own substance.

These years doubtless owe less to the Romantic heritage, which had been already largely absorbed, than to the concerted influence of those two broadcasters on the wave length that will become our modern sensibility: Charles Baudelaire and Gustave Flaubert. In both of them we already find a painful duality, a conflict between the consciousness of an unacceptable reality and the wish to escape toward an impossible paradise.

Salammbô and *Hérodias* long influenced those who went into ecstasies at the end of the century, dreaming of gold and purple litters, languid slaves adorned with chrysoprases, virgins who imbibed moonlight, orgies, stupors, massacres. The other side of Flaubert's personality announces the neurasthenia of the dejected, apathetic characters whose lack of appetite was dissected by the Huysmans of *En Ménage* [Setting Up Housekeeping] and *A vau l'eau* [With the Stream]. A quarter of a century before the apotheosis of Zola and Maupassant, Flaubert made the following agonizing confession to Maxime du Camp: "I had, when I was still very young, a complete presentiment of life. It was something like a nauseating kitchen smell escaping through a vent. One need not have tasted it to know that it will make one vomit." This is exactly the feeling one finds in the literature of the naturalists and their followers. It is true that Flaubert apparently took a certain pleasure in this dereliction: "The ignoble pleases me," he wrote to Louise Colet. "It is the sublime of the lower depths; when it is true, it is as rare as that of the heights." Like Huysmans, Jean Lorrain would have subscribed to this sentence that Georges Bataille found so touching.

Through Baudelaire, whose organ-stops for storm and stress go from the conch-shell murmur of *Une Charogne* [Carrion] to the sulfurous stridencies of the *Litanies de Satan* [Litanies of Satan] and the painful contraltos of Lesbos, the macabre, the diabolical, the saturnine take over the taste of the day.

To indicate how far his influence has gone without his having been responsible for this in any way is not to diminish the stature of the author of the *Fleurs du Mal* [*Flowers of Evil*]. Relaunched by Huysman's *Là-bas* [*Down There*], sterile satanism abounded in the nineties in the innumerable odes to Lucifer and novels dealing with Witches' Sabbaths or Beelzebub.

In private, unbelievable orgies, costume parties, and living tableaux took place, where the queens and princes of the day, theater people, and "ethopoets" mingled. A memorable scandal broke out in 1903: Jacques

[92] An inscription by Verlaine in the glass of a vase by Emile Gallé (1889).

d'Adelsward, the Count de Fersen, was accused of celebrating black masses in his mansion on the avenue de Friedland. They were really "pink masses." Adelsward diverted himself by bringing together schoolboys, who were hardly wild creatures, in his "house of horrors" and having them mime the Death of Petronius or Roman Saturnalia. Liane de Pougy and Émilienne d'Alençon were invited on occasion to these artistic bacchanalia, which were also frequented by Reynaldo Hahn, the director of the Opera, the actor de Max, and Jean Cocteau, at that time a very young man.

The affair caused much talk, and soon a new scandal took its place beside it, that of the "white nuptials," which broke soon after the other and compromised a certain Bulton, an American painter.[93]

In 1906 the Théâtre de la Bodinière announced the production of Roland Brévannes' *La Messe Noire* [The Black Mass], a super-spectacle in ten tableaux, among them one in which naked beauties offered their virginity to Satan and the Abbé Guibourg celebrated the mass on the bare body of Madame de Montespan, and then, in the last act, the "modern orgy" in Adelsward's "house of horrors," in which a nude young man was shown lying on a tiger skin, his arm curved about his head and an ephebus beside him crowning him with roses.

The street itself was thus imperceptibly taken over by the "supreme vice." Even before 1900, the Cabaret de l'Enfer, directed by Dorville, had opened on the boulevard de Clichy. Its waiters were dressed as devils and for a sixty-five-*centime* bock beer, the client had the right to see a "magic" show, interspersed with obscenities.

This era has sometimes been called the "gay" era, and sometimes been considered "sad." François Mauriac reproached it for its stupidity, not admitting that people could applaud Sardou's plays and at the same time hoot at Debussy. But we ourselves have seen some stupid things and will see more; is yesterday's stupidity any worse than today's? Romi, a scholar whose specialty is brothels, called it a "sad era" because of its vulgarity, which in his case, let it be said in passing, is equivalent to biting the hand that feeds

254. Christophe Henri Karel de Nerée tot Baberich. Sepia. 1910. Hessiches Landesmuseum, Darmstadt.

[93] Roger Peyrefitte, *L'Exilé de Capri* (Paris: Flammarion, 1960).

255. *Two Women*. Auguste Renoir. Sketch.
Petit Palais, Paris.
"My body, oh my sister, is suffering
deeply in its beautiful soul!"
Jules LaForgue

256. *Venus and Cupid*. Gustave Moreau. Robert Lebel Collection, Paris.

you. It is true that there is a vulgarity typical of *La Belle Epoque*, a bad taste peculiar to the time, and a baldness of language, a coarseness of manners in everyday life that astonish us today. One would nonetheless have to be quite blind not to see that vulgarity, far from growing less with time, has only changed form, and that there has been no progress as far as public taste is concerned.

It is not our intention to compare these bygone years with our own times. Outside of collective calamities and catastrophes, we

258. *Isis.* Lard. Cf. Comte A. de Villiers de l'Isle-Adam, *Isis,* Paris, (Liège), 1862.

257. Christophe Henri Karel de Nerée tot Baberich: Drawing. 1904. Hessiches Landesmuseum, Darmstadt.
"Yet I feel eyelids closing within me."
Henry Bataille

do not believe that any one era is gayer or sadder than any other: the most that can be done is to try to define its originality.

The thirty years that have occupied us here are characterized by a remarkable moral hypocrisy, whereby the rising bourgeoisie attempts to mask the bitterness with which it defends its privileges and the violence of its appetites. Therefore literature, from the sparkling trifles of André Theuriet or Octave Feuillet to the melodramas of Philippe d'Ennery, was a palliative, in which virtue and goodness were bound to triumph.

The naturalists, more inclined to draw up an inventory of miseries and faults than to look at life through rose-colored glasses, reacted against this insipid idealization of a society which elsewhere behaved cynically.

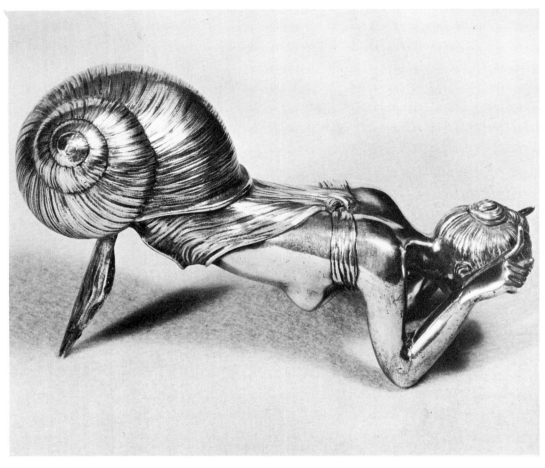

259. Silver umbrella-handle. Circa 1895. Rina Rosselli Collection, Paris.

On yet another hand, esthetes turned away from a reality that was too harsh and sought forgetfulness in mirages.

The age of *froufrou*, of legs flung in the air and of "errant vice," as Jean Lorrain put it, offered a curious blend of triviality and refinement, of cruelty and innocence. Despite the fierceness of the struggles of the time—the struggle between classes and that between generations—the rampant greed of the search for pleasure, and the irritational disordering of the senses practiced by those seeking paradise, the world of Art Nouveau is candid and guiltless.

Later there will be other influences: the tormented heroes of François Mauriac, the restlessness and doubt of André Gide, the anxious introspection of Marcel Proust, and finally Sigmund Freud, whose discoveries will not reach the general public until some time around 1920. Let us not forget that it is in the soil of the turn of the century that these new shoots germinated.

Surrealism is an offshoot of this era in several respects. A noble lineage, that goes beyond the question of mere imitation, links the Chevalier Des Esseintes, Monsieur de Phocas, and Nadja, and this image of André

260. Illustration for Pierre Louÿs's *Aphrodite*. A. Calbet.

"The gold of hair,
The blue of eyes
The flower of flesh…"

Paul Verlaine

261. *Diaboli Virtus (To Saint Augustine)*. Félicien Rops.

Breton's: "My woman with a gladiola for her intimate parts" recalls the insidious charm of a vase by Émile Gallé.

"My flesh is sad," Mallarmé sighed, and eroticism is the thorn in it. This latent pessimism runs like a filigree through all of Art Nouveau eroticism, and the sensuous leap of naiads in silvered metal or dream-Bilitises are attempts to give the lie to it. One remembers poor Lélian and pitiful Paul Verlaine, a weary faun being gnawed away by absinthe and poverty, who exclaimed toward the end of his life: "—Ah, yes, white forms, dripping amber and shadow, despotic, haunting odors, all good, the freshness and the warmth and the dampness and the woven satins, and then delights and white and pink and black and blond and red curls, and the caress of sheets and the resilience of beds and the abandonment of will, not to mention the plunges, into what? Your hands, your lips.... Your body, having recovered somewhat, has an erection once again—and *may someone come who's nice*, may Y or X or Z enter: ah, misery, this is misery, true misery, the only misery...."[94]

Better than many a bravura passage, this long sob of a solitary man tortured by the flesh seems to us to color this era in which everything awakened desire: furnishings, the street, the bundling of women in layer upon layer of clothes, the suggestive license of dances.

There is no need for us to pass moral judgment on times that are still close to us, although they already seem far distant. We shall be satisfied if we have done nothing more than retrace the double profile of Eros and *La Belle Epoque* whose contradictory convulsions—from nausea to perfect bliss—can still move us.

262. *The Satiated Harpy.* Gustave-Adolphe Mossa. 1905. Musée Jules Chéret, Nice.

[94] Paul Verlaine, *Oeuvres Posthumes* (Paris: Albert Messein, 1903).

263. *The Witches' Sabbath.* Sir John Lindsay.
1898. Stephen Higgons Collection, Paris.
"On the edge of her pallid dreams,
she was the one who does not lie,
so greatly was she loved."
Francis Viellé-Griffin

The author would like to express his gratitude to those who have aided him by providing advice, information, and unpublished or rare documents: Lisa Deharme, Annette Vaillant, Rina Roselli, Heanne Adréani, Dorothea Tanning—Paris; Lodewijk Houthakker, Karel Citröen—Amsterdam; Roland Penrose—London; Gerhart Bott, curator of the Hessisches Landesmuseum—Darmstadt; Ernest Goldschmidt—Brussels; Raffaele Carrieri, Franco Russoli—Milan; Bustave Mossa, curator of the Musée Jules Chéret—Nice; André Costa—Toulouse; Jean Waldberg— Saint Martin de Ré; Robert Giraud, Jean Vignes, André Rivage, Robert Lebel, Stephen Higgons, Marquis de Bolli, Félix Labisse, Tristan Tzara, J. M. Capuletti, Jacques Lagrange, Pascal Pia, Jacques Bertrand, Hans Bellmer, Jacques Hérold, François Chapon, Jean Hugues, Maurice Rheims, and Jean-Jacques Pauvert—Paris.

264. Drawing. Christophe Henri Karel de Nerée tot Baberich. 1904. Hessisches Landesmuseum, Darmstadt.